INTERIOR
STYLE
art deco

INTERIOR STYLE
art deco

JENA QUINN &
LUCY DERBYSHIRE

contents

Immerse yourself in the mesmerizing world of Art Deco design, from a time when innovation, youthful exuberance and opulence defined an era. With its geometric shapes, bold lines and lavish ornamentation, the Art Deco movement redefined style and decoration. It permeated the visual world through art, architecture and interior design, reshaping everyday life. It was a statement of modernity and a declaration of progress and the power of human creativity. In this book, we explore the intricate tapestry of design approaches from this elegant era, as defined by precision, sumptuousness and craftsmanship. Whether fashioned by the pioneering masters of the past or the avant-garde creators of today, each interior showcases the enduring magnetism and glamour of Art Deco.

The book begins with a historical exploration of Art Deco's evolution, paying homage to its cultural influences and visionary pioneers. From the iconic works of Émile-Jacques Ruhlmann, Jean Dunand and Jean-Michel Frank to the architectural marvels of New York's skyscrapers and the allure of Hollywood's silver screen, we trace the roots of this iconic design era.

In Chapter Two, we celebrate the diversity of Art Deco design, showcasing exquisite examples that embody its various interpretations and remarkable versatility.

The final section of this book delves deeper into the design principles, offering a professional interior design perspective on how to infuse Art Deco charm into your own home. Unlock the secrets of successful Art Deco interiors and learn how to transform your spaces into contemporary interpretations of this captivating aesthetic.

page 2 *Bold hand-painted stripes in a hallway with an elegant Art Deco vintage pendant, designed by Pierce & Ward.*

previous pages *Virginia Courtauld's iconic vaulted bedroom in Eltham Palace, London, UK. Designed by Peter Malacrida, 1936.*

right *The gilded and luxurious hand-painted 'Deco Dawn' wallpaper by de Gournay, as shown in the de Gournay showroom, San Francisco, USA.*

The 1920s heralded the age of modernity with its unapologetic decadence, innovation and break from traditional values. Following the unprecedented loss of life during World War One and the cruel mortality of the Spanish influenza, those who survived sought to create a new world. In the USA and Europe, youth culture became more visible and influential in shaping social and cultural trends. 'Pleasure was the colour of the time,' noted the drama critic Harold Clurman. This was the era of cocktail culture for a generation immortalized by F. Scott Fitzgerald in *The Great Gatsby*.

Following the war, the Allies, particularly the United States, experienced economic growth, leading to increased consumerism, the rise of new technologies and greater accessibility to luxury goods and automobiles. This modern era was forward-looking and consuming. It was a time defined by speed and progress, celebrating all that was new and

history

optimistic. This fresh visual vocabulary gave rise to a design movement from France that would define modernity and the decorative arts of the twentieth century.

opposite *The iconic lobby of the Chrysler Building, New York, USA, featuring ziggurat-shaped inset lighting and walls in slabs of rich Moroccan marble.*

Arts Décoratifs

As early as 1912, French politicians wished to 're-establish the threatened prestige of the French Decorative Arts' through hosting an international exhibition where only modern works would be displayed. This was realized in 1925 at the Exposition Internationale des Arts Décoratifs et Industriels Modernes, which coined the term 'Art Deco'. In this exhibition, geometry came to represent modernity. The architect Jean Badovici exclaimed, 'Behold the sobriety of line in all the decorative arts! The soul of this geometry must have something to say to modern man.' As with Cubism in the paintings and sculptures of the day, Art Deco redefined the decorative arts through rational geometry and mathematical precision. Here, Art Nouveau's organic curvilinear shapes were replaced by aerodynamic lines, representing machinery and technology rather than nature. As cars whizzed through thriving cities lit with the novel use of incandescent lighting, speed and stream-lined automotive materials became the expression of the design movement. This velocity was visually represented through rectilinear geometry and metallic finishes of gold and chrome.

The discovery of King Tutankhamun's tomb by Howard Carter in 1922 captured not only the public's imagination but also the imagination of artists, designers and architects of the era. The lavish and glittering treasures found in the tomb appealed to the bold opulence and excesses of this period's consumeristic and pleasure-seeking attitude. Egyptian motifs were seen in film, in the visual and decorative arts and on the towering architecture of emerging cities, as well as stylized lotus flowers and falcons, obelisks and stepped ziggurat pyramid designs. These geometric, linear and dynamic motifs became components of the Art Deco movement.

right *Design for a Study, by architect and interior designer Eric Bagge, emphasising a heightened verticality of proportions. Illustration from a brochure for the Exposition Internationale des Arts Décoratifs, Paris, 1925.*

The exhibition of 1925 was a triumph. Pavilions and displays showcasing the era's architectural and artistic philosophies extended from the Grand and Petit Palais, the Esplanade des Invalides and along the banks of the Seine. Reportedly, 16 million visitors descended on Paris over the seven-month run. The architecture, interiors and furnishings from the legendary designers of the exhibition established the design movement, and Art Deco design principles began to spread with an impressive speed worthy of its time. Whether by land or sea, the designers crafted a lavish world of mathematical precision, interlacing geometry and ambitious optimism. Initially reserved for the elite, Art

Deco design found expression in the remarkable architecture and towers of the burgeoning cities, contributing to both the prominence and accessibility of this movement to the broader public. Yet, it was through Hollywood and the silver screen that Art Deco entered the imagination and dreams of millions. These films would not only represent an aspirational and glamorous world for those in the 1920s but also a world of hope and escapism from the decade of turmoil that would follow.

opposite *Les Perruches by Jean Dupas, framed in vibrant marble on walls of silk lampas, in the celebrated music room at the Exposition Internationale des Arts Décoratifs, Paris, 1925.*

above *A bedroom on a barge, designed by Paul Poiret for the Exposition Internationale des Arts Décoratifs, Paris, 1925.*

Émile-Jacques Ruhlmann

Following the global success of his pavilion in the 1925 exposition, Émile-Jacques Ruhlmann became one of the most prolific and sought-after designers of the Art Deco movement. With delicate precision and an eye for purity, balance and form, Ruhlmann decorated and defined all aspects of an interior, from furniture and lighting to textiles, carpets and ceramics, embodying the essence and sophistication of the Art Deco style. His furniture designs are celebrated for their sumptuous materials, streamlined forms, elegant proportions and a sense of understated luxury. His work was both contemporary and timeless, declaring a furniture design perfect when it 'fulfilled need as naturally and simply as possible' while exhibiting the right balance of volume, ornamentation and elegance. This harmony of form and function was equally apparent in his spellbinding interiors, which blended classic proportions with modern fluency.

Born in Paris in 1879, Émile-Jacques Ruhlmann became one of the most celebrated furniture designers of his era. In his youth, Ruhlmann worked alongside his father in the family painting and contracting firm, forging professional links with architects and designers. This early exposure to design and decoration provided practical understanding of form and volume. Ruhlmann embraced the rational simplicity of his era, seeking to create a new movement and style to replace those of the past. Moving beyond the Vienna Secession, Art Nouveau and Arts and Crafts movements, Ruhlmann favoured furnishings produced from luxurious materials with symmetrical designs. His furnishings retained the most subtle and elegant sinuous forms and curves contained within a form of geometric and rational simplicity.

For Ruhlmann, inspiration was found in the neoclassical designs of the late eighteenth century. French furniture makers of the day, known as *ébénistes*, were highly skilled craftsmen working with exotic woods and magnificent marquetry in materials such as wood, ivory and metal. Drawing from ancient Greek and Roman art and architecture, these luxurious eighteenth-century creations were more geometric, symmetrical and restrained than the earlier more ornate and flamboyant rococo style. Some of the most celebrated furnishings from this time were created by the royal cabinetmaker, Jean-Henri Riesener. His furniture was not only celebrated for its exquisite craftsmanship and use of luxurious materials but also for its innovative and functional designs. Therefore, it is no surprise that Ruhlmann's contemporaries referred to him as 'the Riesener of the twentieth century'. As with Riesener, Ruhlmann's work is known for its use of lavish materials, impeccable craftsmanship and innovative designs. Similarly, Ruhlmann's clientele was affluent. Due to the cost of manufacturing and materials, these 'precious' pieces could only be obtained by those with considerable wealth.

above *A design of green, white and gold balanced elegance in this boudoir by Émile-Jacques Ruhlmann for his pavilion at the Exposition Internationale des Arts Décoratifs, Paris, 1925, showcasing his fuseau-legged rolltop desk and finely outlined chairs.*

Ruhlmann's meticulous, artful precision and selection of priceless materials meant that the production cost for every piece of furniture amounted to nearly half the sale price. The remaining half was spent on the development of these detailed designs and paying for the exceptionally skilful artisans he employed. In addition, there were the costly exhibitions that were essential promotional tools to reach his exclusive clientele and to influence public opinion. Ruhlmann believed that the decorators in his craft were similar to couturiers in setting the fashion of the day and that this, as with clothing, could only be achieved by dressing the homes of those who set fashion.

In his furniture design, Ruhlmann strove to achieve sumptuous simplicity. The volume, balance and form of his furnishings blended harmoniously with the luxurious materials, where each detail unfolded on closer inspection without allowing a single feature or adornment to detract from the whole. Ruhlmann had tremendous respect for cabinetmaking and the art of sculpting in wood. He favoured the luxurious macassar ebony and amboyna burl woods for their regular and consistent grains over other materials epitomizing this era, such as lacquer and shagreen. His refined eye and edited sculptural forms required few additions or embellishments. Even in the application of his favourite wood materials, Ruhlmann did not allow the grain to draw the eye away from the overall appearance of the piece. The harmony of geometrical and curvilinear forms and balance of textures and ornamentation created pieces of unrivalled luxurious simplicity.

opposite *A Collector's Study, designed by Ruhlmann, is a stunning display of verticality, with his streamlined fuseau-legged furnishings, including the Nicolle cabinet and Elephant chair, alongside a mural painted by Jean Théodore Dupas, circa 1925.*

left *An elegant cabinet fabricated in amboyna wood with ivory ornamentation, designed by Ruhlmann, 1919.*

Embellishment was deliberate and carefully crafted to work within the balance of the furniture. Despite the technical difficulty, laborious construction process and cost of the materials, the decoration was meant to be viewed intimately and appreciated slowly. The overarching design was not to be compromised. Ruhlmann created rhythm and sinuous movement through decoration, fluting, strips of metal and ivory curves, waves and spirals. The fuseau leg was a lyrical and innovative shape that Ruhlmann designed for his furnishings. Here, Ruhlmann replaced the traditional leg that followed and clearly upheld the structure of the furnishing with this 'spindle' leg. Showing his devotion to, and pursuit of, perfection, it took a week to produce each leg. The fuseau leg was detached from the structure, and with its sinuous geometry, it formed part of the decoration.

Fixed often halfway up and to the side of his furnishings, the effect was to create furniture of such lightness and perfection that the piece appeared to float. It was noted of Ruhlmann's designs that, 'It takes uncommon skill and incomparable sureness of taste to mould these almost imperceptible curves, and to choose the one curve that will give the piece its character and its supreme elegance.'

Character created through the right curve is delightfully apparent in Ruhlmann's Elephant chair. The name is drawn from the shapes and features, which evoke an elephant, distinctively through the chair backrest, which resembles elephant ears in its broad, curved shape. With the Elephant chair, Ruhlmann created a thoroughly modern and whimsical interpretation of the classic armchair, drawing inspiration from Art Deco's fascination with exotic shapes and themes.

opposite *The Tardieu desk, a handsomely crafted demi-lune desk of macassar ebony with gilt bronze details, designed by Ruhlmann, 1929.*

above *Ruhlmann's Fuseaux cabinet in macassar ebony, named for his innovative fuseau leg design. An excellent example of his artistry in balancing form and ornamentation, with complex marquetry in silvered bronze and ivory, finished with tassled handles of silk, circa 1925.*

From his foundation in decoration, construction and furniture development, Ruhlmann refined his instinctive understanding of volume and proportion. Working with the masterful architect Pierre Patout, Ruhlmann moved from the more niche world of his elite clients into the global sphere, through the suite he named the Hôtel du Collectionneur for the exhibition of 1925. Through his collaboration with artisans such as Jean Dunand, Pierre Legrain and Edgar Brandt, Hôtel du Collectionneur was the triumph of the exposition. In this separate structure, consisting of private and entertaining rooms, Ruhlmann 'succeeded in catalysing all the major tendencies within Art Deco'. The oval Grand Salon was the most celebrated of these glamorous rooms. Dedicated to music, the narrative unfolded with paintings on the cupola illustrating Beethoven's symphonies and a stunning grand piano of macassar ebony featuring Ruhlmann's innovative fuseau leg design. Curves and geometrics were juxtaposed, creating a perfect balance between the oval and rectangular shapes of the architecture. Ruhlmann's chandelier resembling a hanging fountain and Gaudissard's curvilinear and flowing carpet design reflected the form of the oval salon and cupola. Both the cupola paintings and the painting above the fireplace, *Les Perruches* by Jean Dupas, continued this interplay and smooth choreography of geometric and curvilinear forms. More rectilinear forms were mirrored in the imposing glazed doors piercing the ceiling border of fluted grey. Here, this geometric dance was visible through the subtle sinuous curve of the light grey silk drapery housed within the architrave. Ruhlmann's meticulous furniture designs continued this rhythmic movement and play of forms with the exceptional Donkey and Hedgehog cabinet that became an icon of his work and the period. In this opulent salon, the balance of colour and form, along with the restrained elegance of Ruhlmann's furnishings, created a harmonious ensemble and re-established both the supremacy of French design and Ruhlmann as the Art Deco designer of his day.

opposite *This oval music room, designed by Ruhlmann for the Exposition Internationale des Arts Décoratifs, Paris, 1925, with his iconic Donkey and Hedgehog cabinet, the grand piano in macassar ebony, a chandelier resembling a hanging fountain, Gaudissard's oval carpet and Jean Dupas's Les Perruches painting above the marble fireplace.*

In his private commissions, Ruhlmann showed a delicate sensitivity for the needs of his clients. In his design, he crafted individual and specific furniture and interiors to represent the client's personal successes and stories. For the study of his client Georges-Marie Haardt, director of the Citroën company in Paris, Ruhlmann celebrated the Croisière Noire (the Black Cruise), a car expedition across the African continent that Haardt participated in with Citroën vehicles. Ruhlmann designed a low cabinet in macassar ebony, oak and silvered bronze; a harmonious study of imposing verticality through wood grain with horizontal construction.

Ruhlmann designed this unique cabinet to complement the impressively scaled painting by Alexandre Jacovleff, representing Zinder, the capital of Niger in West Africa. Furthermore, in his interiors Ruhlmann showed a fascination with, and mastery of, the flow of rooms, from public to private, which allowed him to successfully personalize and curate authentic and unique interiors for his clients. Ruhlmann's delicacy in adapting spaces and furnishings for the function of the room reflected his theory of masculine and feminine harmonies, allowing each room to accommodate different social interactions and varied levels of intimacy.

As with others of his era, such as the American architect Frank Lloyd Wright, Ruhlmann played with the theatricality of volume. By lowering the ceiling height in passageways, Ruhlmann found that he could manipulate the impression of these principal rooms, creating a sense of even greater height and grandeur. Moving from a low to a high ceiling is known to elicit a sense of wonder and awe, imbuing a room with a greater sense of luxury and elegance. This ease with drama and theatricality is variously present in Ruhlmann's interiors. The impression of height is further accentuated by richly grained wall panelling, often in rosewood. Other features that added to this dramatic vertical emphasis included wall fluting and pillars. These vertical techniques enticed the eye upward towards the ceilings, which were often coffered or vaulted for an added spectacle. An excellent example of this effective technique is present in the 1925 hall and salon of Lord Rothermere in Paris, where columns defined these two separate spaces,

opposite *Imposing sculptural columns define the separation of space in this salon Ruhlmann designed for Lord Rothermere's apartment in Paris, France, 1925. The interior reveals an edited and unifying design, with low relief Egyptian themes in the upper panels and an elegant geometric cornice design for ornamentation, creating a room of luxurious simplicity.*

left *Ruhlmann's design for a salon, 1929, showcases his rational and geometric simplicity with lighting and furnishing designs.*

creating an architectural screen. The monumental volume and height of this stunning room were accentuated through an edited and unifying simplicity of the walls and columns, both surfaced in a sumptuous layer of uninterrupted wooden cylinders and wall panels. Elegant and balanced wall ornamentation in low relief, referencing the modernized forms of Egyptian wall paintings, created a decorative ornamentation that complemented the overall design without competing with the quiet nobility of the interior. As with the walls, the sleek dividing columns harmonized with the delicately ornamental and shimmering metallic fluted design at the capital of the column, importing Deco-inspired luxury. For Lord Rothermere, through his unique Art Deco aesthetic, Ruhlmann crafted a majestic interior that was dignified, refined and opulent.

Monumental artwork was another means by which Ruhlmann injected theatrical verticality into his interiors. In the Salon des Artistes Décorateurs in 1926 and the Haardt office in the Citroën works in 1929, Ruhlmann selected strikingly modern and lavishly colourful artwork, highlighting the imposing proportions of these interiors. This technique both accentuated and celebrated the generous height while adding to the sumptuous luxury and geometric affinity that defined the Art Deco movement and Ruhlmann's creations. Lighting further enhanced these cleverly crafted and dramatic interiors. In the Salon des Artistes Décorateurs from 1928, Ruhlmann once more designed an extravagant crystal

chandelier formed by 'strings of pearls' in a controlled and geometric design of three circles gradually reducing in diameter as they rose to a column of crystal pearls. Though, possibly, the most unexpected and modern cinematic addition came from the strip lighting concealed in the dropped cornice, continuing uninterrupted around the oval-shaped stately bedroom. Ruhlmann's lighting designs were seamlessly woven into his interiors and expertly designed in rational geometric shapes. These elegant structures were created from a curated study of simplicity, form and volume and were constructed from the finest materials, such as alabaster with silver and gilt bronze, opaline glass and Sèvres porcelain.

Île de France

Imposing and noble Sèvres porcelain urns on plinth designs of cuboid pedestals created a wondrous impression for those fortunate first-class travellers on the liner *Île de France*. Completed in 1927 and the first liner to be produced after World War One, *Île de France* was also the first to be entirely illuminated through an indirect lighting system and the first where interiors departed from traditional designs and themes of the past. In *The Only Way to Cross*, John Maxtone-Graham stated that this presented 'the divide from which point ocean liner decorators reached forward rather than back'. Following the rapturous and global embrace of the newly coined Art Deco design after the Exposition Internationale des Arts Décoratifs et Industriels Modernes in 1925, the Compagnie Générale Transatlantique, or the French Line, turned to the artists, decorators and artisans of the celebrated exhibition, including Ruhlmann, Pierre Patout and Jean Dunand.

Ruhlmann was appointed to design the first-class Salon de Thé in the reception hall of the French liner, along with the corridors linking the first-class salons, the great hall and the main stairway. In the tea room, Ruhlmann restored verticality to this vast reception hall through 'accentuating the chromatic contrast between the ceiling and the green and pink tints of the marbled ash panelling', as Florence Camard noted in her 1993 book *Ruhlmann: Master of Art Deco*. This theatrical verticality was further emphasized through the repetition of the full-height windows, which were cleverly designed to conceal that the hall was, in fact, below the waterline. Through the use of engraved, frosted and sand-blasted blinds, along with subtle illumination, the design was wondrously effective. These rectangular forms of 'light' were framed on each side by pilasters of ash panelling, continuously drawing the eye upwards. Infusing drama through verticality, Ruhlmann rhythmically placed his Sèvres urns on their ash pedestals along the ash pilasters and walls. Illuminating the shallow, coffered, brilliant white ceiling above through uplighting, these electrified urns served as brilliant modern-day classical sculptures. Through repetition of geometric forms on both the walls and ceiling, Ruhlmann created a room of rational order, overall geometric reason and elegance.

Whether on the 'floating palaces of the Jazz Age' or through his clients' resplendent interiors, Ruhlmann established the tone and narrative for Art Deco design through his meticulous attention to detail, reinvention of classical forms and embrace of the simplicity, vigour and efficiency of his modern era. Despite his early passing at the age of 54 in 1933, Ruhlmann's legacy continues through his dance of sinuous silhouettes and geometry and the luxurious simplicity of his interiors.

above *The Salon de Conversation on the ocean liner Île de France, designed by Pierre Patou in 1926, exquisitely epitomizing Art Deco luxury and sophistication.*

left *The Grand Salon on the ocean liner Île de France, designed by Pierre Patou in 1926, exudes an aura of Art Deco grandeur, showcasing an exquisite blend of lavish ornamentation, geometric patterns and opulent materials that define the era's iconic style.*

Jean Dunand

The Art Deco movement ushered forth a myriad of influential designers whose contributions left an enduring imprint on the era's aesthetics and design principles. In the company of Émile-Jacques Ruhlmann, other forward-thinking visionaries began to explore the essence of Art Deco, epitomizing the fusion of opulence and modernity that defined the movement. Art Deco distinguished itself by its open embrace of diverse expressions and its receptivity to a multitude of varying design approaches. Within this rich tapestry of creative exploration, Jean Dunand emerged as another significant figure within the Art Deco milieu. A contemporary of Ruhlmann, Dunand navigated the same era but embraced a distinctive approach. His background in metalwork and lacquer art propelled him to create opulent designs that stood in contrast to Ruhlmann's minimalist elegance.

Ruhlmann and Dunand offer a fascinating insight into the movement's remarkable versatility as a design philosophy. Ruhlmann's emphasis on simplicity and clean lines exuded a sense of understated luxury, while Dunand's work revelled in ornate and intricate detailing. Nevertheless, rather than serving as opposing forces, their distinct styles made enduring and complementary contributions to the Art Deco movement. Alongside contemporaries such as Jean-Michel Frank, their efforts enriched the epoch, leaving behind a legacy of creativity and innovation that continues to inspire designers and enthusiasts alike. What unites these visionary designers within the broader Art Deco context is their unwavering dedication to the art of craftsmanship. They possessed a remarkable talent for elevating commonplace objects and spaces into exquisite works of art. Their dedication to harmonizing aesthetics with functionality remains a quintessential motif of the Art Deco movement.

Born in Switzerland in 1877, the son of a goldsmith, Jean Dunand embarked on his artistic journey from a young age.

above *This panel illustrates Jean Dunand's mastery of intricate lacquer work, skillfully creating bold geometric patterns with luxurious materials. This exquisite piece serves as a testament to Art Deco's fusion of modernist design principles and exquisite artisanal techniques.*

His path into the world of art and design began with formal studies in sculpture and design at the École des Arts Industriels de Genève. During these formative years, he not only honed his skills but also discovered his passion for working with non-precious metals. It was here that he delved into the intricate craft known as *dinanderie*, a late Medieval metalwork technique that involved embellishing non-precious metals, such as brass, with gold and silver. Through this transformative process, commonplace metals were elevated into exquisite decorative pieces of art.

In his quest for artistic growth, Dunand dedicated his summers to perfecting his craft under the tutelage of a local coppersmith in Geneva, immersing himself in the nuanced art of *dinanderie*. This hands-on apprenticeship enabled him to master the delicate intricacies of metalwork before continuing his creative journey. In 1897, he made a pivotal decision to move to Paris, where he began an apprenticeship with the Art Nouveau sculptor Jean Auguste Dampt. Under Dampt's guidance, Dunand developed an appreciation for the ovular and geometric forms that defined the visual language of decorative arts at the time. Working predominantly with copper, Dunand began experimenting with geometric patterns – a precursor to the flourishing Art Deco style that he would later whole-heartedly embrace. His artistic prowess caught the attention of the Musée des Arts Décoratifs, which, in 1904, made a significant acquisition by purchasing one of his *dinanderie* vases. This solidified his status within the medium, paving the way for his future accomplishments in the world of art and design.

above *A lacquered cabinet by Jean Goulden, 1922, epitomizes Art Deco's fusion of form and function, marrying sleek lines with sumptuous materials in a testament to the era's sophisticated aesthetic.*

opposite *A plate by Jean Dunand, 1912, with a meticulously gilded peacock feather motif, showcasing exquisite craftsmanship and artistic finesse. A lacquered vase, crafted by Jean Dunand in 1924, that exudes a timeless elegance with its sleek silhouette and sumptuous lacquer finish.*

In 1912, as his creative enthusiasm continued, Dunand delved into the delicate realm of lacquer artistry under the tutelage of the Japanese master, Seizo Sugawara. This meticulous craft involved applying layers of refined lacquer as a means of protection and embellishment for his metal creations without compromising their aesthetic appeal. This newfound expertise allowed Dunand to seamlessly integrate the complexities of lacquer work into his creative process, ushering in an additional layer of artistic innovation and craftsmanship into his distinctive style. As his confidence and expertise continued to grow, Dunand delved deeper into his exploration of techniques. He ventured into the prestigious Japanese technique known in French as *coquille d'oeuf*, incorporating minuscule shards of eggshell into the lacquer. This dedication to innovation, coupled with his remarkable aptitude for swiftly mastering novel techniques, gained him increasing acclaim for the exceptional skill and finesse. Through the *coquille d'oeuf* technique, he transcended the boundaries of merely crafting vases and small accessories and ventured into the realm of monumental wall panels and entire rooms, each of them showcasing his exquisite attention to detail. This enabled Dunand to become distinguished not only for his unparalleled mastery of lacquer work but also for his unmatched genius in pushing the boundaries of this art form. His pioneering work played a pivotal role in introducing the art of lacquer into the heart of the Art Deco aesthetic, and his innovative techniques served as a bridge, seamlessly connecting traditional craftsmanship and the modernist principles that Art Deco embraced.

At the 1925 Exposition Internationale des Arts Décoratifs et Industriels Modernes, Jean Dunand made a significant impact, displaying his artistic process and innovative design sensibilities. His artistic vision materialized through a quartet of monumental hammered-copper vases, which stood as imposing examples of his craftsmanship. These vases were embellished with captivating lacquer patterns featuring a harmonious interplay of squares, triangles, chevrons and undulating lines. His artistic approach did not only testify to his impeccable dexterity but also served as tangible examples of the stylistic motif that became inextricably woven into the tapestry of the Art Deco movement. However, it was not solely these masterpieces that captured attention; it was also Dunand's visionary design for the smoking room within the pavilion of the Société des Artisans Décorateurs that left an enduring impression. In this pioneering project, the room's interior continued to feature a stunning array of geometric patterns and motifs, such as angular lines and chevrons. However, he transported the motif onto wall panels, furniture and decorative screens and, therefore, exaggerated the patterns onto a larger and more impressive canvas. The use of exotic woods, lacquer work and polished metals reflected the movement's penchant for luxurious materials. Sculptured panels and low reliefs enhanced the room's three-dimensional quality, while custom-designed lighting fixtures cast a warm, inviting glow. This was the first occasion where Dunand introduced lacquer panels on the walls, foreshadowing the seamless integration of this transformative technique into his future work. In doing so, he captured Art Deco's commitment to merging modernity with opulence, creating a timeless and visually captivating interior that epitomized the essence of the twentieth century.

This triumphant debut served as a prelude to a remarkable commission that materialized in 1930. This commission was no ordinary undertaking: it was the creation of the legendary Les Palmiers smoking room, nestled within the Parisian apartment of

opposite *Two decorative vases designed by Dunand. The first, from 1913, with intricate wisteria motifs and demonstrates his exceptional attention to detail and artistic prowess; the other, from 1935, showcasing refined craftsmanship and his exceptional application of lustrous finishes.*

below *An exquisite lacquered games table with four matching chairs. Designed for the Paris apartment of Madeleine Vionnet by Dunand, 1929, blending meticulous craftsmanship with elegant design.*

Mademoiselle Colette Aboucaya, on the illustrious rue de Monceau. This room, a true testament to Dunand's artistry, has been eloquently described as 'the complete, quintessential Art Deco environment, a fait accompli,' in which Dunand seamlessly blended modernity with elements of formal and cultural tradition. In doing so, he encapsulated the very essence of the Art Deco style.

The walls of Les Palmiers were exquisitely adorned with meticulously crafted lacquered panels, intricately embellished with gold and silver details. These panels showcased a refined fusion of Japanese influences and splendid Louis XV-style gold inserts, creating an ambiance of unparalleled luxury and charm. At the heart lay a central theme – a geometric forest with a pronounced Cubist influence. The result was an abstract yet recognizable composition that enveloped visitors in a dreamlike and ethereal ambiance, perfectly attuned to the seductive allure of a smoking room.

These exquisite panels featured geometric patterns, angular lines, zigzags and repeat motifs, as well as streamlined shapes, such as elongated rectangles, trapezoids and bold curves. These forms created an encapsulating sense of movement and modernity while showcasing a compelling fusion between artistic creativity and geometric aesthetics. Dunand's design approach on this masterpiece seamlessly echoed the design ethos of the era, making it a noteworthy example of Art Deco interior design.

The panels that adorned the room's walls not only showcased Dunand's artistic vision but also demonstrated his unparalleled technical prowess and the exceptional quality of materials employed. What sets these panels apart is their enduring resilience; despite undergoing numerous transfers and subsequent assemblies, they have remained remarkably intact, preserving their original beauty without a hint of damage. These panels are a testament to Dunand's dedication to craftsmanship, which have since been acknowledged and celebrated through various auction houses, finding new homes with the highest bidders.

above *Dunand's Les Palmiers – a smoking room of exquisite design – was meticulously crafted by the artist in 1936 for an apartment in Paris, France. With lavish palm-inspired motifs and luxurious furnishings, it epitomizes the height of Art Deco sophistication and indulgence.*

above *A screen created for the music room of Solomon R. Guggenheim's residence in Port Washington, Long Island, USA. This was a collaboration between Jean Dunand and sculptor Séraphin Soudbinine, 1926, and it stands as a testament to their combined artistic genius, blending intricate craftsmanship and sculptural finesse.*

above *Two captivating panels titled La Chasse (The Hunt), masterfully created by Jean Dunand in 1935, showcase a mesmerising blend of lacquer, gold leaf and paint on plaster. Currently exhibited at the prestigious Wolfsonian Museum in Florida, USA, these artworks immerse viewers in Dunand's intricate craftsmanship and timeless artistic vision.*

The SS *Normandie*

Another pivotal moment in Dunand's illustrious career unfolded during the mid 1930s, when he received a prestigious commission to decorate the SS *Normandie*, a luxury ocean liner celebrated as a masterpiece of Art Deco design. Tasked with transforming the ship's interiors, Dunand drew upon his extensive knowledge of *dinanderie* and the art of lacquering to breathe vitality into the vessel. As a multifaceted designer and sculptor, he immersed himself in every aspect of the project, assuming meticulous oversight of technical systems, production and the intricate details of decoration.
He dedicated the year of 1934 to this monumental endeavour, with his depth of devotion mirroring the grandeur and splendour of the ocean liner itself.

Three of Jean Dunand's most renowned creations aboard the SS *Normandie* were *The Chariot of Aurora*, *The Conquest of the Horse* and *The Return of the Hunters*, all exemplifying his exceptional talent in decorative metalwork and his ability to create an immersive experience for the onlooker. These masterpieces became integral components of the ship's interior design and played a vital role in establishing the liner as the epitome of luxury travel during its era. Today, they are celebrated as iconic pieces showcasing the synergy between Dunand's exceptional talent and the principles of the Art Deco movement.

The Chariot of Aurora adorned the ship's elegant Grand Salon, occupying a place of prominence on the room's focal end wall. In a remarkable collaboration with the accomplished artist Jean Dupas, the piece vividly portrays the Roman goddess Aurora gracefully guiding her celestial chariot across the heavens, showcasing Dunand's exceptional craftsmanship and artistic prowess. Employing a masterful fusion of lacquer, bronze and silver leaf, Dunand achieved a captivating and dynamic effect. The backdrop, bathed in a radiant, golden hue, served as a perfect canvas for the celestial theme, and the skilful integration of silver and bronze added a three-

above *The Grand Dining Room of the ocean liner SS Normandie, circa 1935, exudes timeless elegance and luxury. With its opulent decor and meticulous attention to detail, it stands as a stunning example of Art Deco design and maritime grandeur.*

dimensional quality to the depiction of Aurora and her chariot. The interplay of light on the surface created a mesmerizing spectacle for passengers, elevating the ambiance of the space to a sublime level while contributing to the inimitable opulence that the SS *Normandie* became renowned for.

The Conquest of the Horse, comprising 18 panels adorned in opulent gold and vibrant coloured lacquer, was carved in exquisite low relief. The narrative embarked on a poignant visual odyssey, depicting the historical evolution of humanity and the noble horse. Against a glistening golden backdrop embellished with enigmatic abstract motifs, the panel vividly portrayed two gallant horsemen chasing wild horses in an extraordinary display of artistry and emotion. Dunand's mastery of metalwork and craftsmanship was evident in the intricate details and relief work, showcasing scenes of horseriding, equestrian competitions and the cultural significance of horses across civilizations. By incorporating an array of metals, including the rich hues of bronze and the burnished sheen of copper, Dunand created a mesmerizing work of art that not only appealed to the eye but allowed passengers to be transported through time and culture, bewitched by the storytelling ability of Dunand's vivid tableau. This notion of transporting the viewer and creating a narrative through design is a common theme in Art Deco interiors, as they typically feature elements evoking exoticism, through the use of exotic materials, and escapism, through their sumptuous compositions.

Jean Dunand's unyielding devotion to the *Normandie* was legendary and is exemplified by his awe-inspiring creation of *The Return of the Hunters*. The monumental gold-lacquered screens, soaring to an astonishing height of 6 meters (20 feet) each, adorned the sliding partition between the smoking room and the Grand Salon. The sheer magnitude of the piece was ingeniously conceived to immerse passengers in a sensory experience that left them feeling dwarfed by its imposing presence. To accommodate the towering stature of this masterpiece, Dunand excavated ditches in his rue Hallé workshops and implemented a meticulously engineered pulley system for their handling. In addition to these engineering marvels, he fashioned the screens from a unique concoction he personally developed – a mixture of plaster and earth aptly named 'sabi'. Remarkably, this sabi mixture possessed an exceptional resistance to fire, capable of withstanding temperatures of up to a scorching 816 degrees Celsius (1,500 degrees Fahrenheit) for a duration of two hours.

The grand debut of the SS *Normandie* in 1935 marked an epitome of opulence, innovation and the quintessential elegance of Art Deco in the realm of ocean travel. Within its superb interiors, the very ethos of the movement came alive, bearing witness to an extravagant fusion of ornate detailing, sleek streamlined forms and the opulence of precious materials. In the orchestration of this opulent vision, other creative visionaries, such as Jean-Michel Frank and Raoul Dufy, played significant roles. Frank's indelible contributions showcased his defining principles of clean lines, understated simplicity and the use of luxurious materials. Meanwhile, Dufy, a revered French artist and designer, bestowed the ship's first-class dining room with magnificent vibrant and dynamic murals that captivated the senses.

above *Entitled La Conquête du Cheval (The Conquest of the Horse), this stunning lacquered and gilded panel by Dunand, circa 1934, captures the viewer's imagination with its exquisite detailing and vibrant hues. It stands as a testament to Dunand's mastery, evoking a sense of grandeur and dynamism.*

The Templeton Crocker Apartment

In 1927, both Jean Dunand and Jean-Michel Frank were commissioned, alongside Pierre Legrain and Madame Lipska, by the multimillionaire Charles Templeton Crocker to decorate the interiors of his apartment in San Francisco, USA. This ambitious endeavour entailed the creation of an array of exquisite commissions, including wall reliefs, screens, furniture and accessories, totalling over 400 meticulously crafted objects. Each of these items were expertly fabricated in the ateliers of Paris and transported to the scenic hills of San Francisco. Within this grand project, Jean Dunand assumed responsibility for adorning Crocker's master bedroom, dining room and breakfast room, while Frank undertook the design of the living room and music room. The infusion of French Art Deco at this level was a rarity in the United States at the time and rarer still in San Francisco. The production of these commissions extended over a year, which was followed by a meticulous coordination effort to ship and install the final creations in situ.

In the octagonal breakfast room, Dunand's artistic expertise shone through. He enveloped the walls with lustrous black lacquer panels, each adorned with effervescent bubbles and iridescent Japanese tropical fish. These aquatic wonders appeared to glide beneath a radiant silver light, delicately rendered in eggshell lacquer and casting an enchanting glow from the surface above. 'His panelling for the breakfast room remains unforgettable,' says Benoist F. Drut of the New York gallery Maison Gerard. 'It was not unlike an aquarium: all black lacquer, with exotic fish swimming around.'

Dunand's master bedroom was also adorned with intricate lacquer work, featuring geometric patterns, bold colours and delicate detailing depicting Cubist motifs of a forest landscape. This lacquer work not only added a sense of depth, texture and visual interest to the room but also created a sense of

opposite *A captivating lacquered panel by Jean Dunand, originally showcased by Maison Gerard at the International Fair in New York. Adorned with an enchanting fish motif, intricately rendered to infuse the space with dynamic allure, it showcases Dunand's exceptional skill and invites guests to immerse themselves in its serene ambiance.*

luxuriousness. 'What makes Jean Dunand's work special to me is how he was able to create a chic Art Deco fantasyland with his lacquer panels,' says Jake Baer, CEO of Manhattan gallery Newel. 'The animals and scenes he created had a distinctive Cubist look, which is iconic.' The custom-made furnishings in the master bedroom further underscored Dunand's ability to blend artistry and functionality seamlessly. From nightstands and dressers to the bed frame itself, these pieces featured bold lines and innovative design elements. The bed was executed using Dunand's favoured technique known as *laque arrachée*, in which a final coat of lacquer is applied over a textured layer; in this case, metallic grey over black. By meticulously polishing the entire surface, Dunand unveiled the raised peaks of the black lacquer, creating a mottled yet smooth effect that added an extra layer of visual intrigue to the room.

Within the same apartment, the juxtaposition between Dunand's work and Frank's stylistic approach created a captivating interplay. In stark contrast, Jean-Michel Frank's sitting room may have appeared ascetic at first glance. However, on closer examination, it radiated a profound richness and elegance that shared a striking affinity with Dunand's artistic vision. Frank's innovative choice to envelop the ceiling and walls with parchment created a harmonious balance between modesty and refinement. The room featured armchairs upholstered in smooth and delicate white leather alongside tables, one adorned in bronze and the other

in shagreen, adding to the tactile appeal and overall sense of luxury. Frank employed symmetrical arrangements within his furniture design, emphasizing balance and order; pieces were positioned with one side mirroring the other. The colour palette remained centred around shades of dark yellow, white and brown, while the square armchairs, characterized by their sharp angles and impeccable symmetry, exuded an air of precision. Beneath the surface, an aura of purity, liberation and tranquil solitude permeated the room, revealing Frank's deliberate restraint and aversion to ostentation. Although seemingly understated, the sitting room emerged as a haven of quiet opulence.

Jean-Michel Frank's music room, with its stunning theatre of mirrored walls, exuded a more whimsical and spirited approach when juxtaposed with his restrained sitting room. The mirrors transformed the space by creating an illusion of expansiveness and luminosity, and ingeniously expanded the room's perceived dimensions, infusing it with natural light. In keeping with Frank's artistic tendencies, these mirrors were thoughtfully positioned to enhance the room's aesthetics and functionality. They served as canvases that gracefully reflected the carefully chosen furnishings, creating an interesting visual interplay between the minimalist, elegant furniture pieces and their mirrored counterparts. This interplay added depth and complexity to the overall design, elevating it to a level of refined luxury.

above *In 1927, railway scion Charles Templeton Crocker hired Jean Dunand to design several rooms in his opulent home in San Francisco, USA, including this breakfast room, where he enveloped the walls with lustrous black lacquer panels adorned with effervescent bubbles and iridescent tropical fish.*

Jean-Michel Frank

Amidst the vibrant tapestry of the Art Deco movement, Jean-Michel Frank's career emerges as a beacon of innovation and aesthetic finesse, leaving an enduring imprint on the various realms of design. Despite his lack of formal training, Frank adeptly navigated the artistic landscape, crafting a distinctive style that epitomized the essence of European Art Deco during the 1920s and 30s. Seamlessly blending minimalist interiors with lavish furnishings, he curated a palette of luxurious materials, including the exotic allure of shagreen, the ethereal shimmer of mica and the mesmerizing precision of intricate straw marquetry.

Born in Paris in 1895, Frank's life unfolded within a narrative of paradox and artistic brilliance, all intertwined with the Art Deco movement. From the tragedy of his father's suicide in 1915 to his own untimely demise in New York, March 1941, Frank's biography traversed the tumultuous landscapes of two world wars. Born into wealth, Frank's privileged upbringing and education at the prestigious Lycée Janson de Sailly in Paris, combined with his legal studies, afforded him the opportunity to fully engage with the creative milieu of his era. His wealth facilitated journeys to captivating destinations such as the French Riviera, Spain and Italy, where he was accompanied by celebrated artists and influencers, each leaving an indelible mark on his creative vision. Enriched by these experiences, Frank's design sensibilities matured, paving the way for his iconic contributions to the core principles of the Art Deco aesthetic.

In 1926, Frank embarked on a transformative journey when he forged a profound friendship with Eugenia Errázuriz, a notable figure whose influence would have a huge impact on his artistic trajectory. Errázuriz, a Chilean heiress to a silver-mining fortune, not only served as a friend but also as a mentor. By introducing him to the elegance of eighteenth-century styles and minimalist aesthetics, she became the main catalyst behind his stylistic preference for radical simplicity. Errázuriz famously

above *Exquisite furniture creations by Jean-Michel Frank, meticulously displayed by the esteemed Comité Jean-Michel Frank. Each piece, carefully curated and thoughtfully arranged, embodies Frank's signature blend of modernist elegance and understated luxury.*

stated that, 'Elegance means elimination,' a philosophy that deeply resonated with Frank and guided his creative pursuits. Her discerning eye and refined taste profoundly influenced his approach to design, shaping the direction of his work. In gratitude, Frank acknowledged in 1940, 'Everything I know [more or less], I owe to her.'

Together, they embraced a design aesthetic centred around 'studied emptiness', where essential furniture and carefully curated ornamentation epitomized extreme refinement. Frank's innovative use of space, not merely as a background but as an integral part of artistic expression, underscored his commitment to sharp proportions and extraordinary materials. Their shared philosophy found its expression in Errázuriz's Parisian apartment, meticulously designed by Frank to reflect his minimalist style.

left *A private bar, designed by Jean-Michel Frank for Madame Massard's residence, circa 1931, encapsulating the designer's hallmark style of timeless elegance while reflecting his meticulous attention to form and function.*

Every element was purposefully chosen, ensuring adaptability for various occasions. Soft hues of beige, cream and grey dominated the colour scheme, complemented by luxurious materials such as parchment, shagreen and exotic woods, adding texture and depth.

Frank's artistic curation extended beyond furniture to include artwork and sculptural pieces, further enriching the space with artistic expression and refinement. This fusion blurred the lines between art and interior design, seamlessly integrating both elements as essential components in the creation of captivating spaces. Frank's design ethos

embraced the simplicity and functionality championed by the Union des Artistes Modernes (UAM). His interiors exuded a poetic harmony, interweaving geometric elegance and cultural diversity into every aspect of his creations.

In his personal sanctuary at 7 rue de Verneuil in Paris, Frank's mastery of design was unmistakable. The walls, gracefully enveloped in exquisitely fashioned wood veneers, paid homage to the movement's reverence for opulent materials and exceptional craftsmanship. Reflecting streamlined sophistication, upholstered furniture filled the space, expertly crafted from luxurious natural materials to enhance both opulence and comfort. Adding a final touch of refinement to the living space were low-slung tables with surfaces adorned in intricate patterns of oak, parchment or lacquer. He retained the simplified silhouettes that were becoming fundamental to his design aesthetic, ensuring that the selected materials remained the focal point of each piece.

Frank's unwavering dedication to furniture design culminated in a pivotal moment when he teamed up with Adolphe Chanaux, a master cabinetmaker renowned for his exceptional craftsmanship. Their collaboration, which began in 1930, marked a significant milestone in Frank's career. Chanaux's unparalleled

prowess breathed life into Frank's rectilinear furniture sketches, utilizing an opulent palette of luxurious materials. This alliance empowered Frank to push the boundaries of conventional design, venturing into the realm of avant-garde material experimentation. This enabled Frank to produce truly iconic creations, solidifying his legacy as one of the most influential designers of the 20th century.

One of Frank's most renowned pieces is the Parsons table, originally conceived in the 1930s. This simple yet sophisticated design features a sleek rectangular silhouette with four square legs, crafted from materials like wood or steel. What made the Parsons table revolutionary was its departure from the ornate embellishments prevalent at the time.

left *Jean-Michel Frank's straw marquetry cabinet, circa 1925, blending traditional techniques with modern aesthetics.*

Frank embraced minimalism, focusing on functionality and clean form over decorative elements. This approach was groundbreaking and paved the way for modernist design principles that prioritize simplicity and practicality. Another notable example is his Cabinet. This exquisite storage solution showcases Frank's mastery of craftsmanship and design. Characterized by its geometric shapes, sleek surfaces and discreet hardware, the cabinet exemplifies his minimalist aesthetic. Crafted from high-quality materials such as lacquered wood, parchment or shagreen, each cabinet is a testament to Frank's commitment to excellence in both form and function. Frank's penchant for blending traditional craftsmanship with modernist sensibilities is also evident in his iconic Desk. Featuring a streamlined silhouette, minimalist design and luxurious finishes, this piece embodies the spirit of Art Deco. Its sleek proportions and thoughtful details, such as

left *The library of Yves Saint Laurent's apartment in Paris, France, photographed in 1976. Originally designed by Christian Bérard and Jean-Michel Frank in the 1930s.*

opposite *This desk and chair, designed by Jean-Michel Frank in 1930, are the epitome of elegance. With clean lines and a minimalist aesthetic, adorned in sumptuous vellum, Frank's pieces radiate timeless sophistication, showcasing his mastery in marrying form and function seamlessly.*

hidden drawers and integrated lighting, make it a practical yet visually stunning piece.

His creative prowess also extended into soft furnishing, with his sofa design being a masterpiece of understated luxury and comfort. Characterized by its clean lines, plush upholstery and low-profile silhouette, this sofa redefined contemporary seating. Frank's innovative use of sumptuous materials such as velvet, silk and leather elevated the sofa from a mere piece of furniture to a statement of refined elegance. Its modular design and customizable features made it a versatile addition to any interior space, further cementing its status as a timeless classic. These iconic examples represent just a fraction of Jean-Michel Frank's groundbreaking contributions to furniture design and remain as relevant and influential today as they were during the height of the Art Deco movement.

Frank's inclination for collaboration extended beyond furniture design, as he merged his creative vision with sculptor and artist Alberto Giacometti. Together, they crafted an eclectic collection of accessories encompassing elegant lamps, ornate sconces, sculptural vases, intricately designed mirror frames and sleek console tables. These joint ventures stood as a testament to Frank's relentless pursuit of precision in every facet of interior design.

Throughout his career, Frank cultivated associations with other prominent figures from the beau monde, including Salvador Dalí, Christian Bérard and Emilio Terry. These partnerships served as catalysts, for blending avant-garde creativity with a pioneering spirit, seamlessly intertwining art and design. The resulting collaborations allowed the pieces to surpass mere functionality, transforming them into captivating masterpieces.

By the mid 1920s, the distinctive 'Frank aesthetic' had gained immense popularity, with the designer being in high demand due to his enviable ability to select only projects that resonated with his artistic sensibilities. In 1926, Jean-Michel Frank solidified his standing as France's foremost interior designer by receiving a prestigious commission from renowned art patrons Vicomte Charles de Noailles and his wife, Marie-Laure. Nestled in the heart of Paris, their apartment became a definitive showcase of Frank's unparalleled taste and extraordinary talent for seamlessly integrating artworks and designs by some of the era's most celebrated artists and designers. Within this opulent space, the imaginative creations of Salvador Dalí, the sculptural masterpieces of Alberto Giacometti and the decorative flourishes of Christian Bérard converged, infusing the interior with an artistic vibrancy that transcended conventional boundaries. Frank's design philosophy, rooted in simplicity, sophistication and the harmonious coexistence of contrasting styles, permeated every aspect of the interior.

The apartment exudes timeless elegance, achieved through a delicate balance of modernist aesthetics and classical sensibilities. Clean lines and minimalist forms, reflective of modernism's influence, coexisted harmoniously with classic elements such as Louis XVI-style chairs and ornately embellished consoles, adding a touch of opulence. A striking feature within the apartment was Frank's ingenious application of parchment-covered walls, showcasing his unique design sensibility. Parchment, with its delicate and translucent nature, imparted a soft, radiant allure to the walls, enveloping the rooms in a warmth and inviting glow. The intentionally understated neutral colour palette served as a canvas for the opulent textures of the furnishings, including low-slung tables adorned with intricate patterns and innovative light fixtures, exemplifying the quintessential Art Deco aesthetic championed by Frank. Utilizing exotic woods like ebony, Frank imbued the furniture with a dark and luxurious tone, juxtaposed with unique textures such as shagreen and the subtle colour variation of vellum. This project remains a timeless masterpiece, leaving an enduring legacy that continues to inspire

above *The Grand Salon of the de Noailles residence, Paris, France, designed by Jean-Michel Frank in the 1920s. Meticulously designed, blending sleek lines, luxurious textures and rich colours, illustrating Frank's unparalleled talent in creating environments that seamlessly blend elegance with functionality.*

contemporary designers worldwide. As recently as 2019, *The New York Times Style Magazine* named the Noailles salon one of 'The 25 Rooms That Influence the Way We Design', reaffirming Frank's profound impact on the world of interior design.

In December 1933, Jean-Michel Frank achieved a remarkable milestone as his grand vision materialized within Cole Porter's opulent Paris apartment. The music room, adorned with a silver ceiling, black lacquer arches and a reflective black flooring illustrating a modernist and theatrical flair, received well-deserved acclaim. This extraordinary project earned a prominent place in the pages of French *Vogue*, shining a spotlight on Frank's aesthetic and his unwavering commitment to pushing the boundaries of design.

The music room in Cole Porter's apartment, Paris, France, designed by Frank, 1933. Frank's masterful touch is evident in every aspect of the space, creating an atmosphere that perfectly complements Porter's musical talents and refined taste.

The apartment itself exuded an ethereal and almost mystical atmosphere, with stained-glass windows and decorative arches adorned with ambient white trees lending an almost ghostly charm. Straw marquetry graced the cabinets, while the finest white leather enveloped the sofa, serving as the embodiment of Frank's signature style. As Eileen Gray aptly noted, 'The spare forms of his aesthetic leave no room for a sloppy cut or stitch or edge. No superfluous moulding or applied decoration could be employed to hide the lack of skills of the craftsman.'

Elsa Schiaparelli, a loyal friend and confidante to Frank since her move to Paris in 1922, entrusted him to design two significant spaces, including her personal residences and her professional headquarters. This creative partnership vividly illustrated Frank's unique ability to seamlessly link interior design with the world of haute couture. Schiaparelli's new headquarters and boutique at 21 Place Vendome in Paris, undertaken by Frank in 1934, remains an iconic symbol of their artistic synergy. Frank's masterful use of luxurious materials, clean lines and minimalist forms in the design perfectly complemented Schiaparelli's fashion aesthetic, renowned for its innovative and surrealistic elements.

In the early 1930s, alongside his successful career as an interior and furniture designer, Frank began teaching to share his knowledge and philosophy with aspiring designers. Teaching at the ateliers of the New York School of Fine and Applied Art in Paris, he likely showcased his own furniture designs, with the Parson's table standing out as one of the most iconic examples. Teaching served as more than just a profession for Frank; it provided him with a platform to articulate and refine his design principles, deepening his understanding of his own work. By engaging with students, he may have also strengthened his own mastery of design concepts, as teaching often necessitates articulating and demonstrating ideas to others. Ultimately, teaching played a pivotal role in shaping Frank's legacy, as it enabled him to disseminate his ideas and influence the future of design.

By the mid-1930s, Frank's style ventured from its minimalist and neutral origins as he experimented with bold and vibrant colours. This transformative shift was notably showcased in one of his final major undertakings before his tragic suicide in 1941. Commissioned to decorate the New York apartment of Nelson Rockefeller, one of the United States' most legendary and affluent figures, Frank's reputation in the design world, coupled with Rockefeller's exposure to his work in Schiaparelli's new boutique, led to this prestigious opportunity.

Frank and Rockefeller shared a profound passion for art and culture, which is reflected in the meticulously crafted interiors envisioned by Frank. Within the living room, the woodwork, skilfully installed by Rockefeller's close associate and architect, Wallace K. Harrison, served as a splendid backdrop against which Frank carefully arranged his selected pieces.

This ensemble included armchairs draped in beige silk, tables boasting three tiers of rich blackened pearwood, Giacometti's bronze sconces, elegant ivory coffee tables, dark green leather Hermès armchairs, a commanding pyramid lamp gracing the desk, and Bérard-designed carpets. Among these remarkable elements, the avant-garde carpet emerged as a particularly noteworthy highlight, seamlessly blending into the apartment's audacious interior design. Its meticulously chosen colour palette exhibited impeccable precision, harmoniously complementing the vibrant abstract paintings hanging on the walls, all without overshadowing the room's overall composition. Once again, this highlights Frank's unparalleled mastery of material impact within a space, a skill refined to perfection throughout his illustrious career.

His remarkable ability to blend traditional craftsmanship with modernist principles

consistently resulted in interiors exuding sophistication
and refinement.

Frank's profound influence on interior and furniture
design is unmistakable, shaping the very essence of the
Art Deco movement. His style, characterized by a delicate
fusion of minimalism and luxury, redefined refinement in
design. Through his adept use of materials, he created pieces
that became iconic symbols of the era. His concept of
'studied emptiness' is an enduring elegance that continues
to inspire designers and admirers today. Frank's legacy
transcends mere design; it stands as a testament to his
remarkable talent for capturing the essence of an era and
elevating it to lasting significance.

opposite *The iconic Parsons
table, a design masterpiece by
Jean-Michel Frank in the 1930s.
With its minimalist aesthetic and
emphasis on functionality, the
Parsons table revolutionized the
landscape of Art Deco furniture and
epitomized the core principles of the
movement.*

above *The low table, by Frank in
1926, features gracefully curved
corners, adding a touch of softness
and elegance to its minimalist design.*

New York Art Deco

Jean-Michel Frank and Nelson Rockefeller shared a profound enthusiasm for art and culture, a passion that manifested itself brilliantly in the crafted interiors conceived by Frank. Within the living room, the woodwork, expertly installed by Rockefeller's close friend and architect, Wallace K. Harrison, served as a magnificent canvas against which Frank meticulously arranged his personally curated pieces. This ensemble featured armchairs swathed in opulent beige silk, tables boasting three tiers of rich blackened pearwood, Giacometti's bronze sconces casting their artistic glow, a pair of elegant ivory coffee tables, dark green leather Hermès armchairs, a commanding pyramid lamp gracing the desk and Bérard-designed carpets.

Among these remarkable elements, the avant-garde carpet stood out as a particularly notable highlight, seamlessly integrating itself into the apartment's audacious interior design. Its meticulously selected colour palette exhibited an impeccable precision, harmoniously complementing the vibrant abstract paintings that adorned the walls, all without overshadowing the overall composition of the room. Frank's peerless mastery of material impact within a space remained a skill honed to perfection throughout his illustrious career. His remarkable ability to harmonize traditional craftsmanship with modernist principles consistently yielded interiors that radiated

sophistication and refinement. Additionally, his unmistakable signature, characterized by the delicate equilibrium between minimalism and luxury, and balance of material impact, was a defining trait evident across his myriad of projects, ultimately crystallizing into the embodiment of 'studied emptiness' that defined the Art Deco movement.

The Art Deco movement's most heroic architectural advances were developed in New York, where Nelson Rockefeller spent most of his life, with one of the most spectacular examples bearing his family name: the Rockefeller Center. Arguably, the most iconic symbol of Art Deco modernity was reflected in these towering skyscrapers of the Manhattan skyline. The American skyscraper emerged as the quintessential symbol of 1920s modernity, epitomizing the era's architectural innovation and urban transformation. These towering structures not only redefined the skyline but also symbolized the burgeoning economic and cultural dynamism of the United States during this period. They came to epitomize vitality, youth and unbridled optimism, becoming symbols of the American spirit of innovation and ambition. Though the United States did not participate in the 1925 Exposition Internationale des Arts Décoratifs et Industriels Modernes, the impact of this theatrical and aerodynamic design vernacular appealed to the American sensibilities at a

time when technology provided the opportunity to create buildings of colossal proportions. New York architect Michael Wyetzner noted that the 'invention of high-strength steel, the safety elevator and the subway' allowed for these towers to rise to unprecedented heights. The steel's superior strength and stability, lightness of frame and flexibility, permitted the towers to far exceed previous building altitudes, while the safety elevator introduced new devices such as emergency stop mechanisms and automatic levelling systems to ensure the lifts did not fail and plummet downwards. Most importantly, these safety devices provided confidence, ensuring that people would ascend to the 77 floors above without fear. Lastly, the subway was essential for bringing the broader public into these emerging and vibrant cities, thus producing both the tenants to occupy and the labourers and craftsmen to build these pillars to modernity.

previous pages *Nelson Rockefeller's 810 Fifth Avenue apartment (New York, USA), designed by Jean-Michel Frank in the 1930s, is a testament to Frank's visionary approach to interior design. With its harmonious fusion of modernist principles and luxurious materials, every aspect of the apartment exudes an unparalleled sense of sophistication and refinement.*

above *A recreation of the rug in Rockefeller's apartment, originally designed by Christian Bérard and reproduced by La Manufacture Cogolin.*

opposite *The majestic lobby of Radio City Music Hall, New York, USA, with the verticality of the crystal and brass chandeliers and the mural Quest for the Fountain of Eternal Youth by Ezra Winter, 1935.*

above *Imposing gilded and fluted columns rise to the golden ceiling mural by José Maria Sert, the Rockefeller Center, New York, USA, 1937.*

left *A gilded intaglio relief of the Roman god Mercury above a sea of geometric forms on the Rockefeller Center, by Lee Lawrie.*

The Art Deco imagery that best symbolizes the skyscraper is the ziggurat motif. Architects of the 1920s in New York were governed by the 1916 zoning laws that required multistoried buildings to be stepped back as they rose in height to avoid blocking light to the street below, a restriction the ziggurat pyramid design expertly addressed. The Chrysler building was the first of these iconic and glorious structures to rise from these technological inventions and American expansion. Designed by the architect William Van Alen and commissioned by Walter Chrysler, managing director of Chrysler motors, the Chrysler Building was completed in 1930. Known as 'the tallest building in the world for the shortest period of time', the Chrysler Building was surpassed by the Empire State Building only 11 months later, serving as an example of the ambitious drive and speed that dictated development in this era.

The Chrysler Building is a study of Art Deco dynamism with the ziggurat setback, geometric brick banding and Egyptian and automotive ornamentation. Art Deco's rational and mathematical precision and linear simplicity are present in the white, beige and dark linear bands of the façade's brickwork. The aerodynamic curvilinear arches visible from the greatest height of the glorious tower create a bold and layered harmony with the geometric angles and voids below. Horizontal bands and vertical rectilinear shapes balance perfectly, providing the reassurance of stability. As the Chrysler Building rose to the pinnacle of its greatest height of 319 meters (1,046 feet), Van Alen softened this verticality through the addition of arches, imposing a decorative lightness to the reassuring solidity of the main structure. The most recognizable and celebrated feature of the Chrysler Building is its regal crown of a radiating sunburst pattern, constructed of non-rusting steel. These terraced arches, punctured by triangular windows, form a balanced composition of geometric forms and aerodynamic curves in keeping with the Art Deco narrative.

Van Alen's inspirational artistry and Art Deco proficiency were marvellously represented in the ornamentation of these terraced steps rising to the crown, which referenced both the Chrysler automotive company and the Art Deco celebration of modernity through innovation. Through the subtle variations in the brick, Van Alen designed tyres with fenders and stainless-steel hubcaps. Framing this swirling and vigorous design are enormous, stainless-steel gargoyles that were perfect replicas of the Chrysler radiator caps of the day. These gargoyles were built onsite on the 65th and 66th floors, along with the Egyptian lotus blossoms ornamenting the terraces below.

Where the outer façade is a composition of linear geometry, curvilinear forms and mechanical innovation, the interior is a study of opulent and lavish Art Deco themes rendered through extravagant materials and monumental scale. The Art Deco principle of unity is visible from the expansive entry of glowing and lustrous yellow-hued glass through the repetition of shapes and materials. Here, stainless steel adorns and produces

left *The iconic Chyrsler Building in New York, USA, designed by William Van Alen, is a composition of ziggurat and geometric forms along with stainless steel gargoyles, which are large scale replicas of the Chrysler radiator caps, 1930.*

overleaf *Elevator lobby of Morroccan marble in the Chrysler Building, New York, designed by William Van Alen, circa 1928–1930.*

rhythmic and geometric movement through the pattern created by this theatrical and extravagant entry of translucent glass. A trapezoidal geometric Egyptian motif, seen below the crown, and arches of the exterior repeat at the greatest height of this entrance and on the dark granite architrave. The monumentality and opulent grandeur of this glowing entry opens onto a gilded and glistening interior of Van Alen's Chrysler lobby.

In this magnificent lobby, the tenets of Art Deco design are visible through sumptuous simplicity, dramatic verticality, theatrical lighting and lavish ornamentation. A single tonal simplicity of rich red Moroccan marble on the walls and floors creates a rational order, while the imposing vertical book-matched marble grain emphasizes the impressive proportions of this grand interior. Rectilinear towers of light reinforce the verticality. These inventive pillars of light built into the structure not only glow and reflect off the glistening marble but also uplight the decorative ceiling above. Balancing the heaviness of the marble walls and heroic columns, these glowing geometric forms dissolve the walls they fill. These built-in linear illuminations form pyramids, undulate and rise and fall, creating an animated and dynamic energy, representing a celebration of movement, technology and invention.

The lift lobby is a melody of lavish and glistening finishes fitting for this iconic Art Deco building. With its brilliant, gilded ceiling, lift (elevator) doors are decorated with marvellous marquetry of delicate Egyptian lotus motifs in outlines of steel. Following this continued unifying theme, the lift interiors are a celebration of geometrics created through varied shapes of precious wood veneers within a geometric grid of steel. Repetition of these Art Deco motifs and lavish materials accentuates the rational simplicity and order that balance opulence with metallic finishes and themes of technical innovation. These themes are met in the remarkable ceiling mural of heroic scale by Edward Trumbull, titled *Transport and Human Endeavour*. Reflecting the optimism and progress of the era, Trumbull painted various modes of transportation that represented the acceleration of change for this effervescent Jazz Age. Automobiles, planes and trains are painted along with the innovators, designers and creators of this towering skyscraper and of the swiftly growing Manhattan skyline. The Chrysler Building lobby mural is a testament to the era's belief in progress, innovation and the human spirit's capacity to transform the world through technology and creative endeavour.

Though the Chrysler Building has been surpassed in height in the Manhattan skyline, the theatricality and grandeur of this skyscraper, with its glorious crown, remains a marvel of engineering and design. Van Alen's towering edifice epitomized the spirit of the Roaring Twenties and the industrial prowess of the United States, weaving the skyscraper and the distinctly American style of spirited vigour, ingenuity and invention into the tapestry of Art Deco's elaborate history.

This iconic symbol of modernity, with its

recognizable tower structure and ziggurat setback, found representation in all elements of life, from cigarette lighters and radios to furnishings, paintings, domestic interiors and Hollywood films. The ziggurat was well suited for the silver screen, with its graphic play of light and shadow and monumental scale. This distinctly American architecture appealed to Hollywood set designers, conveying the American spirit and dominance in technology and innovation. Yet it was in Hollywood that the Art Deco message found its greatest global representation. Black and white films of the era disseminated this dynamic and modern ethos to all who could afford a 25-cent ticket. During the 1920s and 30s, Hollywood films provided a glimpse into a glamorous and glittering world. In this black and white dreamscape, the 1920s Jazz Age found expression for its need for reinvention. This luminous world of optimism, hope and, perhaps more importantly, upward mobility provided the ideal escapism from deprivation and crippling poverty of the Great Depression. Incredibly, despite the financial hardships of the 1930s, 85 million people a week watched Hollywood films. Yet, the art director who shaped these aspirational Art Deco worlds was unknown to most in his time and is still largely unknown today, despite having won 11 Academy Awards and designing the coveted golden Oscar statuette.

opposite *Marquetry doors of exotic wood, nickel and brass create fan and geometric patterns on these elevator doors in the Chrysler Building.*

left *The lobby of the Chrysler Building, with imposing verticality, sumptuous materials and innovative lighting.*

Cedric Gibbons

Cedric Gibbons was born in 1893 in Dublin. As the son of an architect, his interest in interiors and art direction was possibly forged through his father's training. Gibbons entered the film industry in 1914 as an assistant to art director Hugo Ballin in New York at Edison Studios. When the studio closed in 1918, Gibbons followed Ballin to Hollywood, where he signed with Samuel Goldwyn in that same year. By 1924, Gibbons had signed with Louis B. Mayer for Metro-Goldwyn-Mayer (MGM) with a contract that reflected Mayer's respect for Gibbon's mastery in his field. Gibbons had inserted a clause stating that his name would be listed as art director for every film MGM released within the United States. For this reason, he is credited as art director for over 1,500 films from 1925 to his retirement in 1956. Though not the sole designer, he defined and oversaw the design of every film, crafting the unmistakable 'look' of the MGM films of his day. In fact, Elia Kazan wrote 'MGM was not run, oddly, by L.B. Mayer, but by the head of the art department.'

An early devotee of the burgeoning design movement forming in France, Gibbons travelled to Paris in 1925 for the Exposition Internationale des Arts Décoratifs et Industriels Modernes. Here, he found inspiration for the luxurious and opulent worlds he would create on film, a new look for a new era. Being the first to replace painted scenery with three-dimensional furnishing, Gibbons drew from the Art Deco visual vocabulary of aerodynamic curves and rectilinear geometry to create his inspired interiors. In these worlds, he often embraced the reimagined American city, flush with possibility, forward momentum and novelty, packaging this particular American optimism for an international audience. Towering skyscrapers, glamorous hotels, decadent apartments and luxurious ocean liners became the settings for his Art Deco interiors.

Art Deco's geometric forms and voids, energized curves and ziggurat steps were perfect mediums for the high tonal contrast of his monochromatic black and white film interiors. Gibbons aptly incorporated these themes on his sets, adding an extra layer of drama through monumental interiors bathed in white. Before 1920, the brutal brilliance of arc lighting was incompatible and blinding when illuminating surfaces painted in white. Due to the advancements in incandescent lighting, this dramatic contrast of black and white was made possible. The Big White Set, or BWS, was a theatrical medium Gibbons perfected in this Hollywood era. For *Dinner at Eight*, Gibbons used 11 shades of white. Jean Harlow's bedroom was a study of white, from the shimmery satin of her sleek clothing to the silken surfaces dressing every surface in her bedroom. Drawing on the opulence of Art Deco interiors, white textural fringe, fur and satin draped and ruffled across the screen, with white satin curtains creating vertical zigzags, highlighting the dramatic contrast of light and shadow.

previous pages *Cedric Gibbons and his actress wife, Delores del Río, in their Californian home of sleek simplicity, designed by Gibbons, 1931.*

left *A still of Jean Harlow on a 'big white set' in Dinner at Eight, directed by George Cukor, 1933.*

opposite *Greta Garbo and Anders Randolf in The Kiss, directed by Jacques Feyder, 1929.*

The theatrical lighting of Art Deco interiors is masterfully woven into Gibbons' sets. Particularly effective are the columns or shafts of uplighting, highlighting the expansive white walls and producing dramatic washes and angles of light upon the actors and their interiors. Lighting became an off-camera character in Gibbons' sets, shifting with ease from sinister to soothing, used alongside shadow to great effect to imbue moral ambiguity and psychological complexity in the characters. In his search for dramatic lighting, Gibbons popularized Venetian blinds, finding these regular divisions of stark, rectangular angles added a sense of mystery and intrigue. The blinds also heightened the realism of the scene, providing depth and a more believable division between the indoor and outdoor world, when the sets of the day were filmed on studio lots. Venetian blinds would become a hallmark of the film noir.

In a still from 1929's *The Kiss*, the last silent film produced by MGM, Greta Garbo and Anders Randolf portray a bitterly unhappy married couple. To represent the emotional chasm between them, Gibbons crafted a stark angular dining room formed from firm linear and geometrical angles. The light bounced and reflected from the glossy black and white flooring, where the two, sitting opposite one another, were framed or bound between bright white strips, portraying the rigid and uncompromising direction and finality of their story. Classic Gibbons white walls were lit upward for dramatic effect, highlighting a sinister circular painting of a ziggurat architectural structure in black and white. Here, the darker tones are particularly foreboding. White and dark shapes were reduced to symmetrical and rigid geometric forms. This minimalist interior created characters of the Art Deco-inspired visual components. The curve of the imposing doors balanced the central black round surround of the artwork. Framing these doors, fluted columns of drapery produced a rigid and vertical symmetry to the scene. More geometric shapes were created in a triangle, formed from

the dark fortress of the artwork to the table beyond, where the two were seated. Though Gibbons created an interior of restrained opulence and wealth through selecting sleek and reflective Art Deco furnishings, the room he designed was as cold and calculating as the relationship the film portrays.

In *Our Dancing Daughters* from 1928, Diana Medford, played by Joan Crawford, was falsely perceived to be a wild and 'modern' young woman. In this Jazz Age romance, the plot turned on this false perception. Appropriately, Gibbons placed Diana's character in the first Art Deco interior on film, highlighting this

'modern' perception of her unreliable character as a fast-paced flapper. Balanced and sumptuous simplicity defined these sleek interiors. In the lobby, the luminous white wall decoration drew from the Art Deco vernacular with vertical fluting of the staircase and walls, and ziggurat steps in the arched door architraves. Stacked fan-shaped chrome wall lights, reminiscent of the Chrysler Building pinnacle, symmetrically framed the scene. The fluted line dynamically curved from the foreground to the staircase beyond, portraying the rapid movement and vibrant energy of this era. Art Deco's unapologetic, bold and adventurous shapes and ornamentation defined Diana's apartment. Rectangular pedestals sat like columns along walls, housing strikingly dark and light angular sculptures and classical urns. Ziggurat forms lit and adorned voluminous interiors of white walls with contrasting pilasters in uncluttered rooms. A press release for the film read, 'Modernistic effects in furniture and architecture are being used with a vengeance by Metro-Goldwyn-Mayer in Joan Crawford's new picture.' Referencing the innovative new furnishing styles, the press release continued, 'Weird beds, almost on the floor, have little woodwork frame save foot-high boards, which conceal the springs and do away with the conventional legs of a bed. These are set against a wall whose only ornamentation is the shape of the doors. Black statues set against gold papered panels form the only ornamental note.' Through these early publicity announcements, this modern Art Deco vernacular was introduced and presented as the defining principles for this youthful and golden decade.

Gibbons artfully mirrored the spirited and vigorous character of the heroine, Diana Medford, through this vital and energized modern decorative style. The film was an enormous success, further establishing Art Deco as the embodiment of the modern aesthetic. Gibbons later noted that *Our Dancing Daughters* created a terrific impact, not only in making the American home more liveable and attractive, but in influencing the work of other film art directors.' During his reign as art director of MGM, Gibbons produced his own cinematic language through Art Deco principles, showing how everyday objects and rational simplicity in decoration could be used to enhance storytelling through visual means.

Of these imagined worlds, Gibbons' most personal project was the home he designed in 1930 in the Santa Monica Hills, where he lived with his wife, the Mexican-born silent-film star Dolores del Río. Upon entering his private domain, rational simplicity and linear order set the stage. Here, Gibbons recreated his Big White Set both indoors and out. Art Deco film motifs were woven into his private world, forging Gibbons' own elegant domestic theatrical style. From the road, a pathway of stone tiles and grass grouting recreated the reflective black and white tile grid of his set interiors. The exterior was a study of balanced geometry formed by stepped rectilinear and square

forms, largely uninterrupted by windows.
The entry door, with its exaggerated ziggurat
architrave, become part of this melody of
angles. Framing the entry wall was a larger
zigzag stepped pattern, which further
balanced the rectangular planes and voids of
the fixed and cantilevered structure. Windows
continued the angular theme on the more
private façade of the house, which flooded
Gibbons' interiors with brilliant southern
California sunlight. Here, Gibbons punctured
the white geometry with various scaled
steel-cased windows and terraces with linear
rails, mirroring both the horizontality of the
architecture and of the window casings. The
overall effect is a timeless, confident and
ambitious building of sleek linear modernity.

above *A set from Our Dancing Daughters,
the first Art Deco interior on film, directed by
Harry Beaumont, 1928.*

For his Santa Monica residence, Gibbons exhibited his fluency and ease with both interior design and art direction, working within the tenets of the Art Deco design movement. Through this thoroughly modern and assured design aesthetic, Gibbons crafted a luxurious and luminous future, not only in his own residence but for each filmgoer and dreamer then and now who enters his black and white stories, wishing to become glamorous heroes or heroines for a few golden hours.

The ziggurat stepped motif appealed to Gibbons' cinematic eye for the way this motif captured light and shadow through use of solid and void forms. Lighting once more played a vital role in his interior. Through the expansive rectangular panes of glass, rectilinear geometric shapes cast shadows throughout the rooms from dawn to dusk, serving as cinematic Venetian blinds. Fitted modern and incandescent light fixtures provided evening drama, both bathing the rooms with light but also dramatically uplighting the various stepped ceiling and wall motifs, which accentuated the contrast between light and shadow.

Gibbons adeptly recreated his modern look from the film screen through the generous use of white paint, shiny black linoleum floors, glossy black marble and reflective mirror. Other modern finishes included metallic chrome and brushed steel, associated with automotive streamlined aerodynamics and luxury liner glamour. The brushed steel staircase joining the ground and first floors was a fine example and fit for film. This staircase, backlit by full-height windows, cast linear dark and light shadows worthy of Gloria Swanson and her closeup. Theatricality, a pillar of Art Deco design, was also present in the interior layout. Bucking traditional architectural norms, Gibbons, with the help of architect Douglas Honnold, designed the main living room on the second floor, ensuring the public space had both expansive views and brilliant light. Here, his cinematic art direction crafted a sense of awe and wonder for his guests and continues to direct these emotions today. Madeline Stuart, the celebrated California interior designer, restored this exceptional residence for her fortunate clients. Speaking with *Veranda* magazine, Stuart said, 'It is such a surprise when you come up those stairs and see it. It's one of the most spectacular rooms I've ever seen.'

left *Dolores del Río at the house designed by her husband, Cedric Gibbons, circa 1935.*

In Conclusion

The Art Deco movement etched a profound and enduring narrative on the world of interior design and the cultural landscape of the 1920s and 30s, while extending its influence far beyond. This era was characterized by an exquisite mélange of stylistic nuances, all intricately woven together, drawing inspiration from modernity and opulence. The movement's diverse expressions across various mediums gave rise to a harmonious interplay of artistic discourse, where key figures within the Art Deco vocabulary not only enriched the collective design consciousness but also forged innovative alliances, all pulsating with the rhythm of creativity and ground-breaking thought.

Visionaries such as Ruhlmann, Frank, Dunand, William Van Alen and Gibson expanded the horizons of artistic expression, intricately shaping the Art Deco aesthetic into the inspiring design movement we admire today. It is worth

below *The first-class smoking room on the SS France ocean liner, 1961, which André Arbus designed in Art Deco style with dynamic sunburst ceiling fixtures and motifs from antiquity.*

opposite *André Arbus's sketch of a dressing room design, 1935. A room of soft elegance, with furnishings of refined simplicity in a room of theatrical porportions.*

casting light on the myriad of other Art Deco visionaries whose contributions have also woven the intricate fabric of this aesthetic, including Raoul Dufy, Armand-Albert Rateau, Louis Süe, André Arbus and André Mare, to name a few. The movement's pioneering initiatives branched out into diverse realms of art and design, with its influence permeating from the intimate corners of interior spaces to the grandeur of architectural marvels and the captivating frames of Hollywood's golden era. The legacy of the Art Deco movement stands as a testament to the transcendent power of design, its capacity to encapsulate the essence of a zeitgeist and its unwavering ability to continue to ignite the sparks of imagination among interior designers, architects and artists to this day.

Art Deco interiors continually captivate with their harmonious blend of style and functionality. Within the upcoming pages, we embark on a journey celebrating outstanding Art Deco designs, each presenting a unique interpretation of the era's rich stylistic spectrum. Some designs exemplify the Art Deco ethos of refined simplicity and understated luxury, while others showcase intricate ornamentation. For instance, the grand entrance hall of Eltham Palace stands as a testament to symmetrical composition and exquisite craftsmanship, utilising exotic woods to stunning effect.

In a contemporary vein, Nicole Fuller's exploration of lacquer work delves into vibrant colours and rich saturation, infusing spaces with a modern Art Deco allure akin to a jewel box. Meanwhile, Alidad's reflective masterpiece, crafted through the decorative mirror technique of *verre églomisé*, offers

showrooms

a mesmerizing interpretation that upholds Art Deco's tradition of fine craftsmanship and opulence.

These diverse examples not only capture the essence of Art Deco but also serve as timeless inspirations, inviting us to appreciate the enduring elegance and innovation of this iconic design era.

opposite *For his Kips Bay showhouse in Dallas, Texas, USA, Ken Fulk's clever design deftly captures both Art Deco's spirit and opulence in this gilded and reflective study and bar, aptly named A Study in Optimism. Pivotal to this sumptuous interior is the exquisite de Gournay wallpaper, inspired by the legendary designer Jean Dunand. This luscious paper emulates Dunand's era-defining lacquer-and-metal panels for the SS Normandie ocean liner. The desk further embodies Deco themes through the luscious lacquer finish, with aerodynamic ornamentation in the chrome legs.*

right *Swedish designer Rolfe Engstromer created this exquisite entrance hall for Stephen and Virginia Courtauld in the 1930s, for their residence, Eltham Palace, London, UK. Luxurious exotic blackbean veneer and marquetry lined walls depict landscapes from Italy and Scandinavia, with a Viking and a Roman soldier introducing symmetry and order to the evocative design. The cylindrical pierced dome design adds brilliant luminosity and imposing scale to this interior, while elegant and simple furnishings are cleverly arranged in a circular layout, a geometric play that mirrors the dome above and captures the natural light.*

above and opposite *Though dating from the 1800s, Pitzhanger Manor in London, UK, designed by the famed architect Sir John Soane, exhibits qualities that have made this exquisite home an inspiration for Art Deco interiors. Sir John Soane was celebrated for his innovative use of space and light, drawing on principles of symmetry, proportion and geometrical and ancient classical forms and ornamentation. In this library and breakfast room, Soane's monumental proportions crafted through bold colours and marble blend with his inventive play with geometric and domed forms and sumptuous finishes to result in a timeless interior.*

previous pages *The gifted designer Tim Gosling chose the Pitzhanger Manor library to showcase his exquisitely crafted Paris Deco rug. There is an interplay of opulence with elegant simplicity through the luxurious yet unadorned wooden walls and mirror. The graceful niches and the central mirror contrast curved and rectilinear forms, with a perfect balance of classic proportions and symmetry that creates a distinctly modern interior. For this reason, the library made the ideal setting for Gosling's Art Deco-inspired furniture collection, showcasing his eye for purity, balance and form.*

left *In Claridge's Painter's Room bar, London, UK, designer Bryan O'Sullivan crafted an oasis in pastels, true to the hotel's Art Deco history. To transport the visitor to the cocktail age, O'Sullivan used graceful geometrical forms in lighting designs, with aerodynamic wall lights, Egyptian fan shapes and a Ruhlmann-style uplighting in the scalloped cornice. To complete this luxurious and timeless interior, O'Sullivan added a pink fluted marble bar with curved walls cleverly decorated with monochromatic Cocteauesque murals by the artist Annie Morris.*

right *The brilliant Madelaine Stuart designed the interior of legendary set designer Cedric Gibbon's home in Santa Monica, California, USA. Stuart retained the original features of the ziggurat stepped wall and mirror, built-in furnishing, glistening black linoleum and cinematic white paint. To these features Stuart added sleek, streamlined furnishings and luxurious materials to highlight the forms and shapes of the seating arrangement. With this interior's interplay between light and shadow, and rational geometry, the home continues to represent Hollywood Art Deco modernism.*

overleaf *This lavish apartment in Paris, France, was designed by Jacques Grange for Yves Saint Laurent and Pierre Bergé and was inspired in part by Jean-Michel Frank's exceptional apartment for Marie-Laure and Charles de Noailles. Grange, well-versed in the Art Deco vernacular, applied his talent to this exquisite interior. With vast wooden walls and large sheets of mirror to help expand the space, Grange fashioned a framework from which to house the magnificent and extensive art collection curated by St Laurent and Bergé.*

right *The Atlas Bar in Singapore was designed by the Hwang family to reflect the dynamic and magnificent structures, and vibrant optimism, of the Roaring Twenties. Hassell Studio collaborated with the family to produce this celebration of Art Deco design, complementing the monumental architecture with geometrical forms faced in luxurious materials such as gilded brass and lacquer. Lighting of chevron and rectangular shapes illuminate the interior, with uplighting highlighting the impressive gilded ceiling fresco, reminiscent of the energy and innovation of a New York skyscraper.*

overleaf *The talented designer Alexandre Lamont fashioned an elegantly refined interior in this residence in Mahanakorn, Thailand. Lamont transformed this wall of wardrobes using a tableau of limed exotic wood and luxurious metal. Art Deco's vitality and movement is cleverly referenced through the white brilliance in the grain of the wood and the pattern on the doors. Playing with light and shadow by using the reflective floor and mirrored ceiling above, this geometric interior exemplifies the modern opulence of Art Deco.*

right *Alidad created a dreamy forest of mirror in this lavish dressing room in London, UK. This enchanting wood was created through the technique of verre églomisé, a means of decorating glass from the back with gold or metal leaf applied to engraved designs. By lining this jewellery box of a room with full-length walls of verre églomisé mirror, Alidad fashioned a space of restrained opulence with sumptuous materials and elegant proportions, embodying the essence and sophistication of the Art Deco style.*

overleaf *Naomi Leff's 1997 living room in New York, USA, beautifully epitomizes Art Deco's core principles. It features exquisite Anigre wood panelling, sourced from Africa, which provides a flawless backdrop. Classic Art Deco wall lights cast an elegant glow that harmonizes with the sleek Macassar ebony furniture, adorned with luxurious leather upholstery. Tall, narrow windows, characteristic of the era, enhance the room's grandeur and scale. Meticulous attention to detail ensures that opulent materials take centre stage, encapsulating the refined opulence synonymous with Art Deco interiors.*

right *This opulent dining room by Nicole Fuller in New York, USA, is beautifully captivating. Green lacquer envelops the walls and ceiling, casting a mesmerising jewel-box effect, while its glossy surface enhances luminosity and sophistication. The deep green tones, intensified by the reflective finish, saturate the space with vibrancy and luxury. Harmonized by matching green upholstery, the design achieves total visual cohesion. Exotic woods and mirrored Art Deco motifs offer elegant contrast to the bold colour, and a timeless Deco pendant acts as the crowning jewel to the space.*

overleaf *This vibrant colour scheme, curated by Greg Natale, beautifully blends a contemporary flair with classic Art Deco principles. Luxurious wallpaper, reminiscent of Dunand, envelops this home in Melbourne, Australia. The harmonious blend of pink and gold seamlessly extends across the walls, upholstery and carpet, creating a cohesive atmosphere. Geometric patterns add precision and elegance, infusing the room with dynamism. Brass accents hint to Art Deco's opulence, while the play of light on metal surfaces injects further energy into the space.*

previous pages *Cartier's flagship store in New York, USA, has an exquisite sense of scale achieved through masterful material selection by Laura Gonzalez. Exotic woods clad the principal wall and full-height sliding doors, accentuating the signature Art Deco proportions. Metal accents showcase meticulous attention to detail, and a decorative lacquer panel in an adjoining room pays homage to Dunand's aesthetic and the era's use of opulent materials. Art Deco-inspired wall lights adorn upholstered walls, further enhancing the overall aesthetic while providing luxurious illumination, further encapsulating the essence of Art Deco design.*

opposite *The lobby in the Fairmont Peace Hotel, Shanghai, China, designed by Hirsch Bedner Associates, embodies Art Deco's devotion to geometric precision. The intricate patterns not only provide visual interest but also establish a harmonious flow, directing focus towards key features. The thoughtful placement of patterns manipulates spatial perception, enhancing the sense of grandeur typical of the era. The interplay of lines and shapes fosters a sense of openness while reinforcing the importance of form and line in the Art Deco aesthetic.*

left *This captivating bathroom by Miles Redd in his townhouse in New York, USA, embodies Art Deco's emphasis on scale and material. Through strategic reflection, the mirrors visually expand the room, elevating the sense of luxury and grandeur. Linear reeded elements within the mirror further enhance the room's height while creating a rhythmic balance with symmetrical proportions around the room. Dark marble flooring complements the mirrors, enhancing reflective qualities and enveloping the space in an enchanting light.*

right *The exquisite metalwork adorning these double doors designed by Studio Eleven exemplifies the transformative power of Art Deco motifs in interior design. Against the white panelled backdrop, the bold metalwork commands attention, effortlessly guiding your gaze upward and accentuating the sense of height. The deliberate narrow proportions of the doors further accentuate this effect. Complemented by pops of colour and accents of exotic wood, the design masterfully captures the era's creative interplay of form, line and sumptuous materials.*

overleaf *The beautifully restored Union Station in New York, USA, is a quintessential example of Art Deco's ingenious use of pattern. The floor's luxurious marble patterns are impeccably scaled to accentuate the room's grand proportions. Diagonal emphasis on the floor extends to the dado tile work, adapting the scale seamlessly. Golden accents are punctuated by the white plaster decorative overdoors, highlighting Art Deco's appreciation for craftsmanship and bold contrast. The central furniture piece seamlessly continues the surrounding pattern play with its sleek geometric lines, epitomising elegant simplicity.*

left *This exquisite bathroom, designed by Steven Gambrel, epitomizes the Art Deco principles of symmetry, showcasing a masterclass in composition. Through the symmetrical arrangement, a feeling of coherence is instilled, ensuring every element in the space contributes to the unified composition. The geometric pattern on the floor enhances a central axis while showcasing the creative impact of a pattern motif and the strategic use of space. The rich veining of the dark marble adds a touch of grandeur, while its paler counterpart complements the era's preference for bold contrasts.*

overleaf *This captivating dressing room, designed by Kelly Wearstler, showcases the era's use of metal and mirror. The interplay of these reflective materials bathes the room in a luminous glow, accentuating its depth and allure. Geometric motifs, meticulously repeated through line and shape, exude precision throughout the space. Contrasting brass tones are punctuated with dark accents, intensifying the visual drama. This contrast extends to the adjacent bathroom, where a striking patterned floor further amplifies the Art Deco aesthetic.*

Whether searching for cinematic Hollywood glamour, the vitality and innovation of New York in the Roaring Twenties or early 20th century Paris interiors, this chapter details the themes and key elements to create your own world of timeless sophistication.

Geometric patterns and motifs add visual language to various forms of decoration, whether through large-scale architectural endeavours or smaller gestures in fabrics and accessories. Exotic woods offer various opportunities to infuse warmth, luxury and refinement to an interior, from lining walls to furnishings. The sumptuous materials of straw marquetry, vellum and lacquer can be brought into an interior in striking and imposing panels, on furnishings, or through small yet effective statements from accessories such as lights. Also available in large or small scale, marble provides a lovely means of adding sophistication, movement and colour. Mirror is a

elements

more affordable element with impressive scale, adding high impact, light reflection and an expansion of space.

As jewellery in a home, lighting provides a useful means of adding streamlined Art Deco forms or geometric opulence. Furniture affords flexibility in design, mixing elements such as exotic wood, sumptuous materials, mirror and marble with a variety of Deco-inspired elegant furnishings. Flooring further combines elements such as geometric motifs, wood and marble, adding vibrant and bold colours or more elegant and refined geometric simplicity.

In this chapter, we will delve into the various methods to create impact with these marvellous materials and features.

opposite *This beautiful bathroom by Robert Passal showcases de Gournay's Namban wallpaper exquisitely, with an abstract seascape in a tarnished 3D gold leaf pattern. The design references the work of Dunand with its clever interplay of swirling coils and graphic lines.*

Patterns & Motifs

Art Deco is characterized by its emphasis on geometric forms, which exude precision and elegance. Incorporating such patterns not only adds visual interest but also establishes a sense of rhythm and harmony within a room, drawing attention to focal points and imbuing interiors with character and intrigue.

Geometric shapes such as zigzags, chevrons and angular lines are quintessential Art Deco motifs, infusing spaces with dynamism and depth. Rectangles, squares, circles and triangles contribute order and symmetry, with patterns like the 'Greek key' providing continuity in contemporary settings.

To achieve balance, designers often juxtapose strong-lined geometric shapes with softer circular elements, enhancing visual depth and harmony in a room. While geometric patterns can emphasize visual flow, care must be taken not to overwhelm the space. Strike a delicate balance by harmonizing the shapes and sizes of furniture and decor. Patterns featuring triangles can inject energy into a room: repeated equilateral triangles, for instance, add depth and dimension, lending a dynamic modern feel to the space. By combining different shapes and forms, designers can create imaginative and inviting environments.

Understanding the principles of geometry and their application in design is essential for achieving both aesthetic appeal and functionality in interior spaces. Patterns and motifs can be strategically utilized to manipulate the perception of space, making small rooms appear more spacious or infusing larger spaces with warmth and intimacy. Patterns with linear elements such as stripes or geometric designs can elongate a room by drawing the eye upwards, making the ceiling appear higher and the walls taller. This helps to open up smaller rooms with low ceilings and create a more expansive ambiance. Conversely, running a pattern horizontally can visually widen a space. This technique is useful in narrow rooms, where it helps to counteract the sense of confinement and create a more open atmosphere.

opposite *Hand-painted stripes adorn the walls and ceiling in this beautiful hallway by Pierce & Ward. A stylized Art Deco pendant hangs prominently above a Milo Baughman table, creating a contemporary twist on the Art Deco backdrop.*

above *Geometric patterns adorn the double doors in Eltham Palace, revealing the exquisite entrance hall beyond. The use of pattern creates precision, dynamism and ornamental luxury synonymous with the era.*

Exotic Woods

Exotic woods hold a magnetic allure in interior design, blending the opulent elegance of Art Deco with the contemporary sophistication of modern aesthetics. Sourced from distant corners of the globe, these rare woods infuse warmth, character and timeless beauty into interior spaces, making them a coveted choice for designers and homeowners alike.

The primary appeal of exotic woods lies in their intrinsic beauty and natural variation. From the deep, rich tones of mahogany to the intricate grain patterns of zebrawood, each wood brings its own unique personality and charm to a space. Whether adorning floors, furniture or architectural accents, they possess a luxury and exclusivity unmatched by common materials.

Macassar ebony boasts a striking appearance with deep black or dark brown colouration, interspersed with contrasting lighter stripes. Its lustrous surface, often polished to a high gloss, further enhances its allure, while bold stripes evoke drama and sophistication. Similarly, zebrawood, aptly named for its graphic stripes, makes an equally bold visual statement. Walnut burl and bird's eye maple are known for their intricate swirls and burl and offer a highly decorative appearance through a different pattern. Used primarily in veneers and marquetry, these visually interesting woods can be used alone or in combination, celebrating the wood's natural movement and colouration through every application.

Exotic woods present unique challenges in craftsmanship compared to more common varieties, due to their density, hardness or distinctive properties. Crafting furniture or decorative elements from these woods demands a heightened level of skill, precision and attention to detail. Artisans specializing in working with these woods often rely on

right *The playful composition by Jean Luc Lemée combines 1920s leather chairs with Joe Colombo 'Elba' chairs, continuing the brown hues of the exotic wood walls while sitting in front of a beautiful brass-detailed fireplace.*

time-honoured techniques such as hand carving, inlaying, marquetry or veneering to bring out intricate details, imbuing furniture and architectural elements with the depth and dimension synonymous with Art Deco.

In contemporary interiors, designers frequently turn to exotic woods to create statement pieces that serve as focal points within a room. These pieces not only showcase the natural beauty of the material but also highlight the incredible craftsmanship inherent in working with exotic woods. Whether it's a meticulously carved console table, an intricately inlaid cabinet or a veneered wall panel, each piece crafted from exotic wood becomes a testament to the artisan's skill and the material's inherent allure.

Another benefit of using exotic woods in interior design is their versatility and adaptability to a wide range of design styles and aesthetics. While traditionally associated with Art Deco, exotic woods can also complement modern and minimalist interiors, adding warmth and texture to sleek, contemporary spaces. Whether used in a traditional panelled library or a minimalist interior, exotic woods bring a sense of sophistication and luxury to any environment.

The use of exotic woods also offers sustainable and eco-friendly options for interior design. Many exotic woods are sourced from responsibly managed forests or reclaimed from salvaged sources, making them a sustainable choice for environmentally conscious designers and homeowners. By choosing exotic woods over more traditional materials, designers can create beautiful interiors that are not only visually stunning but also environmentally friendly.

While exotic woods may come with a significant price tag, they can be used sparingly or lavishly, depending on budget constraints and the design vision. Whether applied in modest accents or as lavish full-height panelling, paired with polished metals or luxurious fabrics, exotic woods continue to embody the essence of Art Deco principles. In both instances, the aesthetic allure of the wood remains paramount, drawing the eye and accentuating its financial and aesthetic value within an interior setting.

opposite *Elegant stairs from the Entrance Hall of Eltham Palace, London, UK, illustrates exquisite figurative marquetry, allowing the viewer to traverse through a timeless realm of sophistication and cultural richness.*

Straw Marquetry

Straw marquetry, a craft dating back to ancient Egypt, gained popularity during the Art Deco era and continues to enchant contemporary interior designers with its timeless elegance and unique aesthetic. This technique intricately arranges thin strips of straw to create patterns and designs on surfaces, such as furniture, walls or decorative objects, blending rich craftsmanship history with a modern aesthetic.

A key aesthetic benefit of straw marquetry is its ability to evoke a sense of luxury and sophistication. The natural texture and warm tones of straw add depth and richness to any space, creating a visually striking and inviting

atmosphere. The intricate patterns and designs created through straw marquetry offer endless possibilities for customization, allowing designers to tailor the technique to suit a variety of design styles and preferences.

The quintessential sunburst motifs, characterized by rays radiating from a central point, evoke optimism and glamour, making the pattern ideal for adding drama and focus in modern interiors.

Straw marquetry seamlessly bridges the gap between the past and the present, offering versatility in contemporary interiors. While rooted in Art Deco, its use in modern design projects adds a fresh and unexpected twist that resonates with today's aesthetic sensibilities. Its timeless appeal and ability to complement a range of design styles, from classic to minimalist, make it a sought-after choice for infusing character and charm into spaces. Due to its level of popularity, many of the world-renowned wallpaper suppliers have developed more affordable solutions and offer exquisite wallpapers emulating the straw marquetry aesthetic in a more cost-effective way.

left *A beautiful curving screen, enhanced by its abstract silhouette adorned in silvered straw marquetry, meticulously crafted by Antonio da Motta for Alexander Lamont.*

opposite *The Ajiro Sunburst wallpaper by Maya Romanoff showcases an elegant sunburst motif, crafted using a classic hand-inlaid technique, delicately applied with micro-thin wood on a paper backing.*

This has inevitably expanded its accessibility, further fuelling its popularity among designers and homeowners alike.

Incorporating straw marquetry into interior design also promotes sustainability. Harvested from renewable sources, straw is biodegradable and enhances the natural connection between occupants and the environment. This eco-friendly alternative to traditional materials aligns with the growing demand for sustainable design practices, contributing to a more environmentally conscious approach to interior design.

opposite *Studio QD's captivating interior showcases a custom scaled and coloured starburst motif wallpaper by Fameed Khalique, complemented by luxurious rust coloured upholstery. Mimicking traditional marquetry, the wallpaper incorporates dye-cut natural paulownia wood, offering tactile richness and unparalleled opulence.*

left above *A tall Amadeo cabinet designed by Alexander Lamont, enriched with jade and celadon tones of straw marquetry, featuring cast burnished brass accents along the top edge and base, evoking the texture of natural straw.*

left below *An exquisite five-folding screen crafted in straw marquetry, designed by Jean-Michel Frank in 1925.*

Vellum

Vellum, a translucent and versatile material crafted from animal skin, seamlessly blends historical charm with modern elegance. With its origins tracing back to ancient times, vellum gained prominence during the Art Deco era for its luxurious texture, which evoked an ambiance of sophistication.

A primary aesthetic advantage of using vellum lies in its ability to diffuse light, creating a soft and ethereal ambiance. Its translucent nature allows light to permeate gently, illuminating spaces with a subtle yet deep, warm glow. This makes vellum particularly well suited for light fixtures and decorative screens, where it can produce captivating visual effects.

Additionally, vellum's texture and natural variations add tactile interest. Wherever it's used, vellum bestows a touch of elegance and refinement upon any space. Its versatility also allows a myriad of design possibilities, from intricate embossing and engraving to sleek, minimalist applications.

Vellum is also functional: its soft, porous surface absorbs sound, reducing noise and enhancing acoustics. When applied to larger areas, vellum can be arranged in panels, reflecting the size and shape of the hides from which it is crafted. Traditionally sourced from calves, goats or sheep, vellum panels exhibit natural colour variations, contributing to the material's aesthetic allure. These panels, arranged in a grid formation, create dynamic compositions within a space, accentuating the beauty of vellum while adding depth and texture to the environment.

opposite *Alexander Lamont revitalizes an iconic Art Deco silhouette, infusing it with a subtle blend of natural parchment and speckled shagreen panels. The addition of patinated solid brass feet adds a touch of timeless elegance.*

above *Custom vellum panels grace the walls and integrated joinery of Studio QD's Dining Room, infusing the space with warm hues and captivating textural luxury. The texture contrasts elegantly with the linear grain of the walnut table, creating an interplay of curves and lines.*

Lacquer

Lacquer, a glossy and resilient finish derived from the sap of the lacquer tree, offers a plethora of aesthetic benefits in interior design. With roots tracing back to ancient China and Japan, lacquer surged in popularity during the Art Deco era for its opulent sheen and capacity to imbue surfaces with depth and richness. Today, lacquer remains a compelling choice for designers, seamlessly transitioning from Art Deco-inspired interiors to modern spaces.

A primary aesthetic advantage of lacquer lies in its ability to create a sleek and polished look that instantly elevates the ambiance of a room. Its high-gloss finish reflects light beautifully, infusing spaces with a sense of glamour and sophistication. Whether adorning furniture, cabinetry, or architectural details, lacquer adds a touch of luxury and refinement, enhancing the overall aesthetic appeal of any space.

Due to its reflective quality, designers can confidently experiment with a darker and more saturated colour palette without the risk of darkening the space too dramatically. The glossy surface acts as a mirror, bouncing the light around the room and creating an illusion of spaciousness. Darker colours with a high gloss finish evoke a sense of depth and richness that is unparalleled by matte surfaces, enhancing the saturation of the colour and imbuing it with vibrancy and luxury. This depth adds dimension to the space, elevating its visual appeal and exuding sophistication.

The combination of dark colours and high gloss lacquer creates a dramatic contrast that adds visual interest to a room. The glossy

surfaces catch and reflect the light, generating dynamic highlights and shadows that accentuate architectural details and design elements, resulting in depth and complexity that captivates the eye and leaves a lasting impression.

From a maintenance perspective, lacquer's inherently smooth and non-porous surface makes it easy to clean and maintain. Resistant to dirt, grime and fingerprints, it ensures the vibrancy and lustre of the underlying colour remains intact over time, making it an ideal choice for high-traffic areas or spaces prone to moisture and humidity.

opposite *Lacquered sideboard, designed by Émile-Jacques Ruhlmann, 1930. A sleek, timeless example of Art Deco elegance.*

above *A 1930s French cabinet in striking orange-red lacquer, curated by Steven Gambrel, defines the space with its vibrant hue. It exemplifies the lavish materiality characteristic of the era, while commanding attention as the room's centerpiece.*

Marble

Marble is closely intertwined with the Art Deco aesthetic, imparting luxury while creating a strong geometric and dynamic linear pattern through its natural veining. Another appealing feature of this ancient material is in the varied and luscious colouration, which celebrates the Art Deco fondness of rich and high contrast tones and impressive ornamentation.

Marble is an excellent means of accentuating height and volume through the use of large-scale slabs. Continuing with Art Deco themes, walls of marble slabs impart theatricality, monumentality and opulence. Book-matching large slabs is a beautiful technique where a block of marble is cut into sequential slabs. These slabs are then arranged side by side, like an open book, allowing the veining and patterns to mirror one another seamlessly. This effect bestows a harmonious symmetry and highlights the unique and luxurious individuality of marble's tones and veining.

Marble can be run horizontally, vertically or in various patterns, creating a more energized and active design. Selecting a horizontal linear direction creates the impression of greater width in a room, as horizontal lines draw the eye to the width of a space, visually widening the interior. Conversely, a vertical linear direction draws the eye upward, creating a sense of height and spaciousness. This is particularly impressive and effective in interiors gifted with generous volume and ceiling height.

For a more economical solution, tiles of various sizes can be purchased in a wide range of marble varieties. To add the Deco tenets of drama and bold geometrics, tiles of the same scale can be laid in alternating vertical and horizontal directions, imparting a playful and vivacious energy to an interior. For additional theatricality, marble slabs can be shaped in various forms, from generous curves to ziggurat pyramid configurations, providing an energized or dramatic design motif for the room.

Marble can elevate surfaces throughout the house, such as kitchen worktops, table surfaces, flooring and walls. When polished, the luminous lustre of marble adds sophisticated glamour; when honed, the result is more streamlined and modern. There are also practical considerations with marble. A honed finish is often favoured for flooring, as this more porous finish is less slippery, whereas a polished finish provides a more robust surface that is less susceptible to staining. Whether honed or polished, marble's dramatic veining and lustrous colouration lend a Deco-inspired elegance and luxury.

opposite *Calacatta viola marble surrounds the walls and sink of this sumptuous bathroom in Mayfair, London, UK, by Studio QD. The horizontal dynamic veining and wall of mirror expands space while a faux painted marble ceiling adds to the theatricality.*

opposite *In this opulent bathroom in Madrid, Spain, by Lorenzo Castillo, dark, luxurious marble framed by a wooden border creates the stunning ornamentation of geometric and ziggurate Art Deco shapes.*

above *Arabascato marble with impactful grey veining creates waves of dynamic movement in this stunning bathroom in Notting Hill, London, UK, designed by Maddux Creative, with accents of luscious antiqued brass adding to the Deco essence.*

Mirror

Mirror has remained a coveted decorative tool since its inception. In addition to its practical use in daily life, mirror amplifies both natural and electric evening light. Placed strategically and symmetrically to balance asymmetrical doorways and windows, mirror enhances the interior's architectural symmetry. Opposite windows, or at the end of corridors, mirrors reveal their luminous versatility through providing an illusion of infinite space. These tools of reflecting exterior views and light and enhancing architectural forms and alignment were embraced by the Art Deco movement.

Mirror can be shaped in various geometric forms, providing streamlined and symmetrical angularity or fluid movement to an interior, from curvilinear shaping to a starburst design. Mirror frames further define the decorative intent through both scale and finish. With Deco-inspired materials – whether aerodynamic chrome and stainless steel, or the more luxurious lacquer, inlaid wood or gold and silver leaf – a mirror frame can either impart modern sophistication or opulent theatricality.

Mirrored walls are marvellously impactful and can provide various decorative results through the use of either plain, coloured or antiqued mirror, or verre églomisé. Antiqued mirror provides a hazy, cloudy finish to emulate the natural aging of mirror, whereas verre églomisé adorns through a means of decorating glass from the back with gold or metal leaf applied to engraved designs. It is through this variety of scale, decoration and finish, along with the almost magical illusion of space and dazzling light reflection, that mirror enhances an interior and elevates the finish of any room in one's home.

right *An elegant mirrored wardrobe for a townhouse in London, UK, designed by Alidad, creates a graceful and delicate woodland through the technique of verre églomisé.*

opposite *Miles Redd designed this stunning and marvelous antique mirrored bathroom for his townhouse in New York, USA – a room of sheer opulence, glistening surfaces and endless reflections.*

above *In this elegant bathroom designed by Studio QD, reflective walls of mirror and patterned lacquer create a rich sumputousness, with accents of antiqued brass and black lacquer adding to the opulence.*

Lighting

Lighting is one of the most important and often-overlooked aspects in the home. Lighting sets the mood in a room, enhances functionality and highlights decorative details. Lighting, in fact, highlights whatever it illuminates, whether intended or unintended, and when employed correctly curates a personal and evocative experience. Through the luminous gaze and focus of lighting, one can create dramatic effects and add depth and layers to a room, emphasizing textures and tones.

The Art Deco designers favoured innovative and modern forms, through a symmetrical play of curvilinear and geometric silhouettes. These designs formed a myriad of shapes, from sleek symmetrical and tonal simplicity fashioned from alabaster and frosted or etched glass to more ornate and lavish forms in crystal and tinted or stained glass. Monumental chandeliers in moulded glass, in geometric and stylized floral shapes, are typical of the era. Theatricality here is expressed through fashioning these materials in a large, imposing scale of rational geometry, intended to make a statement.

Metals in bronze, brass, chrome and brushed steel framed and outlined the ornamentation. These materials were often polished or lacquered to a brilliant reflective sheen to complement the era's celebration of sleek lines and modern technology. Working in bronze, the celebrated Swiss sculptor and painter Alberto Giacometti created some of the most ethereal and textural lighting of the era. Giacometti's lighting designs were modelled after figures and forms that resembled his haunting and iconic sculptures, drawing on nature as a backdrop for their vulnerable fragility. Despite their delicacy of design, Giacometti's lighting designs are impressive, striking and unarguably modern. Jean Royère was another celebrated lighting designer who created elegant and artful designs with an innovative use of metal. Metal in his hands took a more playful and curvilinear form, at times painted in vibrant colours and in a variety of textures.

Lighting in plaster defines the Deco era. Appreciated for its versatility, affordability and the ease with which it could be moulded into intricate shapes, plaster linked innovation and functionality with artistry and luxury. Giacometti's designs are the most collected and reinterpreted for their interplay of geometrical forms with textural richness, illuminating and decorating some of the most celebrated interiors today.

opposite above *In the Painter's Room at Claridge's, London, UK, BOS Studio designed this geometric interplay of cylindrical forms with stepped designs of chevron and rectangular bands.*

opposite below *Art Deco theatre lighting adds to the drama and dynamism of an interior through a large canopy of bronze and frosted glass geometric shapes and stepped bands of semi-circular fans.*

left *Lampe Tete de Femme (Head of a Woman lamp), designed by Alberto Giacometti, circa 1937.*

below *Plaster wall lights designed by Alberto Giacometti for the Villa Noailles, Hyères, France.*

opposite top *Lustre avec Femme, Homme et Oiseau (Chandelier with Woman, Man and Bird) in bronze, designed by Alberto Giacometti, 1949.*

opposite below *Persane eight-armed wall light, designed by Jean Royère, circa 1953.*

Furniture

Art Deco furnishings are sought after for their sleek, geometric lines and elegant simplicity, which reflects the favoured modernity and technological progress of the era. The use of luxurious materials – such as exotic woods, lacquer, inlaid ivory and polished metals – brings sophistication and glamour to these direct and graphic forms.

The shape and comfort of seating and upholstery define a room's decorative intention and functionality. For a Deco feel, there are several forms to draw from to provide that instant era-defining glamour. Émile-Jacques Ruhlmann's Elephant chair exhibits exaggerated curvilinear comfort with sumptuous wood details. This dramatic shape is best covered in single-tone fabrics or leather to avoid detracting from its balanced geometry.

In modern upholstery, Deco design is found in the linear simplicity and clear geometry of shapes, with the addition of luxurious materials. These materials complement and harmonize with the structure, creating a balance between form, fabric and precious materials, as represented in the Mirador lounge chair artfully crafted by Alexander Lamont.

Whereas, for a more sculptural detail, Paul T. Frankl's Skyscraper chair celebrates the vibrant and spirited energy of this time. Frankl's chair is a melody of angles and ziggurat steps, finished in lacquer and silver leaf to represent the metallic details of technological and automotive innovation.

For both form and function, furnishings by Jean-Michel Frank remain some of the most celebrated and reproduced designs of this era. Frank's designs are characterized by clean lines and a lack of ornamentation, focusing instead on luxurious materials. He chose sumptuous materials that were pale and unadorned for elegant simplicity.

For his hard furnishings, Frank favoured lavish materials such as shagreen, parchment, leather and rare woods, which elevated his simple geometric lines to artful forms. Employing similar materials, Ruhlmann's designs remain contemporary. His desks, tables and consoles are favoured for their streamlined, symmetrical and harmonious designs. Both Frank's and Ruhlmann's designs can be purchased today, with various interpretations available on the market. Key features for Deco furnishings include bold shapes, simple geometrical forms and luxurious materials, ensuring that the fabric selected for upholstery balances harmoniously with the design.

opposite *Sideboard of rectangular forms in contrasting luxurious woods, circa 1930.*

above *Red lacquer and silver leaf finishes on wood for the Skyscraper chair, designed by Paul T. Frankl, circa 1930.*

opposite above *Simple elegance in the Galeria daybed, designed by Antonio da Motta for Alexander Lamont.*

opposite below *Gracious curves and geometrics in sumptuous materials form the Mirador lounge chair, designed by Antonio da Motta for Alexander Lamont.*

Flooring

Flooring provides another opportunity to showcase bold geometric patterns, luxurious materials and striking visual contrasts. Balancing the interior design and colours in a room is key to the success of including these more vibrant and dynamic shapes, ensuring that one element does not overpower another. Through colouration and ornamentation, flooring complements Art Deco interiors' rich finishes, furnishing and lighting designs.

Geometric patterns provide the dominant visual language of Deco flooring. Patterns reflect the fascination with modernity but also the look back to ancient civilizations through such shapes as zigzags, sunbursts, chevrons and stylized floral motifs.

High tonal contrasts and linear geometry suit the luxurious materials of stone, marble, granite, terrazzo and inlaid wood. A play of geometry can be highly effective through a combination of these materials. In the interior by the acclaimed designer Kelly Wearstler, a study of geometric shapes and scale produces the predominate ornamentation in the room. Here the tonal curation and balanced furniture composition compliments this energized and dynamic flooring. The legendary Hollywood set designer Cedric Gibbons favoured the geometric and tonal graphic of black and white tiles. This design is both impactful and comparatively easy to implement.

The more elaborate patterns are particularly successful in carpets and rugs, meticulously designed to create a sense of balance and vibrance to an interior. Christian Bérard and André Arbus are two designers who developed masterful

right *In this former 1940s warehouse-turned-residential loft in Soho, New York, USA, designed by Kelly Wearstler, geometric flooring leads the ornamentation in this luxurious and spirited interior.*

creations during this period, and wonderfully both are still represented through the French carpet manufacturer Cogolin. Bérard's rugs reflect his work as a painter, set designer and illustrator. Due to his unique eye, his rugs are more painterly in nature, with a whimsical and surreal aesthetic, combining bold patterns, floral motifs and figurative elements, whereas André Arbus favoured a more unifying and holistic design and geometry. With these diverse motifs and tonal variations, rugs and carpets provide an affordable and relatively easy means of introducing Art Deco's theatricality and geometric symmetry to bestow an interior with the desired opulence and modernity.

opposite *Geometric and elegant simplicity in the Élysée rug from the Arbus Collection, by La Manufacture Cogolin.*

above *This André Arbus-designed Aubusson rug, circa 1940, with its bold tones and geometric elegance, was part of the Karl Lagerfeld collection in 2001.*

Index

ACKNOWLEDGEMENTS

Jena Quinn and Lucy Derbyshire would like to thank:
Karen Howes of Interior Archive for her genius and artfully curated visual library
Lisa Dyer for her calm and patient brilliance and expertise
Isabel Bass for her constant beloved friendship and support
Their families for their unwavering support and love.

PICTURE CREDITS

The publishers would like to thank the following for their kind permission to reproduce the images in this book.

Cover images: © Stephen Karlisch, courtesy of de Gournay (front); © Ricardo Labougle (back)

AKG Images CDA/Guillemot 52–3; De Agostini Picture Lib./G. Dagli Orti 32l; Les Arts Décoratifs, Paris 79, 155; Les Arts Décoratifs, Paris/Jean Tholance 31l, 31r, 78; Picture Alliance/Photoshot 147t; Sotheby's 134; VIEW/Dennis Gilbert 84; VIEW/Andy Stagg 85; WHA/World History ArchWHAive 32r. **Alamy** Art Collection 3 37; Cultural Archive 17, 19; Everett Collection Inc 73, 76–7; Gabriel Parra 65; Hemis 146b; History and Art Collection 38–9; imageBROKER/Chris Putnam 114–5; Mascheter Movie Archive 71; mauritius images GmbH 108; Nathaniel Noir 126. Penta Springs Limited 13, 15, 36; Peregrine 63b; The Archives of the Planet 12. **Alexander Lamont** 96–7, 122, 128, 131t, 132l, 132r, 151t, 151b, 154. **Anson Smart** 104–5. **Bridgeman Images** Archives Charmet 10–11, 27t; Christie's Images 18, 25, 33, 34–5, 41, 43, 49, 57, 92–3, 131b; Diltz/Metro-Goldwyn-Mayer Pictures 72; Historic England, 4–5; Minneapolis Institute of Art/The Modernism Collection, gift of Norwest Bank Minnesota 150; NPL – DeA Picture Library 30; NPL – DeA Picture Library/Etude Tajan 28–9, 51; The Estate of Alberto Giacometti 146t; The Stapleton Collection 21, 23, 24. **Claridges** 88–9, 145t, 158. **Comité Jean-Michel Frank** 47, 54–5. **de Gournay** Alexandra Shamis 6–7; Stephen Karlisch 81, 121. **Feau & Cie** 22. **Getty Images** Angelo Hornak 66, 68; Bruno Perousse 63t; Herbert/Stringer 62; Heritage Images 82–3, 123; Print Collector 16, 27b; Stuart C. Wilson/Stringer 147b; Tony Evans/Timelapse Library Ltd 149. **Interior Archive** Annie Schlechter 152–3; James Macdonald 98–9, 140–1; Mark Luscombe-Whyte 124–5; Ricardo Labougle 110–1, 142; Simon Upton 138. **Joe Thomas** 9, 69. **La Manufacture Cogolin** Franci Amiand 61. **Maddux Creative** Ricardo Labougle, 139t. **Maya Romanoff** 129. **Pearce & Ward** Matthew Read 2. **OTTO Archive** Björn Wallander 102–3; Eric Piasecki 116–7, 135; Max Kim-Bee 90–1; Roger Davies 118–9; Scott Frances 100–1, 106–7. **Shutterstock** MGM/Kobal 75; Pascal Hinous/Condé Nast 50; ThelmaElaine 145b; Wallace Woon/EPA-EFE 94–5. **Studio Eleven** Liza Gurovskaya 112, 113. **Studio QD** 130, 133, 137, 143. **The Rockefeller Archives** 58–9. **The Rug Company** 86–7. **Thérèse Bonney Photographs, the Regents of the University of California, The Bancroft Library, University of California, Berkeley** 45. **Wikimedia Commons** Taylz468 56.

opposite *The private dining room of the Foyer and Reading Room, Claridge's, London, UK. The striking artwork of the 1920s 'flapper girls', with the opulent glass and geometric forms, overwhelming evokes the Art Deco era.*

First published in 2024 by OH
An Imprint of HEADLINE PUBLISHING GROUP

1 3 5 7 9 10 8 6 4 2

Cataloguing in Publication Data is available from the British Library

Hardback ISBN 978-1-83861-214-6

Printed and bound in China

HEADLINE PUBLISHING GROUP
An Hachette UK Company
Carmelite House
50 Victoria Embankment
London EC4Y 0DZ

www.headline.co.uk
www.hachette.co.uk